ACCOUNTING ETHICS

ACCOUNTING ETHICS

A Practical Guide for Professionals

Philip G. Cottell, Jr.,
and
Terry M. Perlin

QUORUM BOOKS
New York • Westport, Connecticut • London

Library of Congress Cataloging-in-Publication Data

Cottell, Philip G.
Accounting ethics : a practical guide for professionals / Philip G. Cottell, Jr., and Terry M. Perlin.
p. cm.
Includes bibliographical references.
ISBN 0-89930-401-X (lib. bdg. : alk. paper)
1. Accountants—Professional ethics. I. Perlin, Terry M. II. Title.
HF5657.C687 1990
174'.9657—dc20 89-24366

British Library Cataloguing in Publication Data is available.

Library of Congress Catalog Card Number: 89-24366
ISBN: 0-89930-401-X

First published in 1990

Quorum Books, 88 Post Road West, Westport, Connecticut 06881
An imprint of Greenwood Publishing Group, Inc.

Printed in the United States of America

The paper used in this book complies with the Permanent Paper Standard issued by the National Information Standards Organization (Z39.48-1984).

10 9 8 7 6 5 4 3 2

CONTENTS

ACKNOWLEDGMENTS

On a warm spring day two college professors met on the sidelines of a field upon which their sons were engaged in a game of soccer. One was a conservative professor of accountancy; the other a liberal professor of interdisciplinary humanities. Surely these two men could have nothing in common other than the sport in which their sons were engaged. Yet during the conversation of that afternoon, a single word emerged that led to a long and rewarding collaboration. That word is *ethics*. One of the results of our collaboration on ethics is the book you have before you.

We are thankful for our opportunity to learn from one another. Each of us believes that his perspectives have been broadened and enriched by our work together. We are grateful to those who made our efforts possible. We would like to acknowledge the support we received from the Alumni Teaching Scholars Program at Miami University. This program offered us the time and the space for our collaboration to begin and to grow. We were nurtured by the supportive atmosphere created by the Alumni Teaching Scholars Program and the opportunity to test some of our ideas in several of its forums.

We also acknowledge the financial support that we received from the John E. and Winifred W. Dolibois Faculty Development Fund at Miami University to work on joining accounting and ethics. Administrative support for which we are grateful came from Lois Simmons, Julie Schlicter, and Norma McClure. Jodine Bonacci was especially helpful during the editing phase of the process.

Finally we acknowledge the moral and spiritual support that we received from our families while we worked on this book. We are pleased to dedicate this book to them.

INTRODUCTION: BEING ACCOUNTABLE

"Does your accountant owe his loyalty to you or to the law?" This question was posed in *Newsweek* during the summer of 1989 in response to an emerging court case that involved a St. Louis CPA's relationship to his client, a pizzeria owner. From 1982 to 1985 the CPA performed auditing and other tasks for the pizzeria owner and received more than $50,000 for his services. At the same time, the accountant was secretly giving details of his client's financial life to IRS special agents. The pizzeria owner was eventually indicted on charges of tax evasion. His attorney argued that accountants should respect client privacy and sued the CPA in federal court.

The attorney argued that "a client has a right to feel he's getting undivided loyalty and confidentiality from his accountant." Many believe that codes of professional conduct in accounting—including the American Institute of Certified Public Accountants (AICPA) code—sustain the attorney's contention. The prosecutor in St. Louis disagreed and stated that "the accountant has a moral and legal obligation to turn over information."[1]

Conflicts of value, disagreements about codes and regulations, and dilemmas of loyalty are encountered every day by professionals. Among other duties, accountants are pledged to truth telling and have clear responsibilities to exercise good judgment and honesty in their professional work. But what happens when professional duties come into conflict with moral principles? And how, indeed, are accountants to sort out such problems, no less resolve them?

Accounting Ethics faces such issues head on. This book does not argue that there are absolute rules of conduct for accounting professionals that will answer all dilemmas. It does, however, claim that identifying moral conflicts, thinking them through, discussing them with colleagues and others, and utilizing the tools of ethical analysis are useful, in fact indispensable, activities. This book raises questions we face every day. Looking at concrete situations realistically, it asks us to reason together about such problems as the CPA who acted as a "double agent" for the IRS.

This book is designed for professional accountants and for those who are studying to become professional accountants. It presumes that the reader is concerned about being (or becoming) an excellent accountant. It also presumes that the reader wishes to contribute to the work of the profession as a whole and to achieve recognition for efforts at behaving ethically and responsibly. *Accounting Ethics* takes its subtitle seriously: *A Practical Guide for Professionals.*

Business ethics, of which accounting ethics is a subspecies, is no longer an esoteric academic enterprise. One can expect to find discussions of ethical conflict in the *Wall Street Journal* or on the nightly news with increasing regularity. Over 90 percent of business schools in this country now offer business ethics courses. Business ethics consultants are in demand by corporations. Many major firms have ethics committees. And we are only at the beginning of a clear trend in the media in exposing white-collar crime.[2]

As W. Michael Hoffman has put it: "Clearly, the ethical thing to do is not always in the best interests of the firm."[3] To state this truism is not to solve a problem, but to present a set of challenges. How are individual accountants to think, and act, when they encounter moral conflicts? How can persons act as professionals and retain integrity? How can the profession as a whole respond to challenges when values conflict?

In this book, we use the terms *ethical* and *moral* interchangeably. We try to avoid jargon and to stimulate thought and discussion in ways that can lead real accountants to face real issues. *Accounting Ethics* is a book about practical ethics, that is, "about the application of ethics or morality . . . to practical issues like the treatment of racial minorities, equality for women . . . and the obligation of the wealthy to help the poor."[4] In an introduction it is also fair to state what a book is not. First, this is not a rule book: it does not provide sure guidelines for all imaginable events. Second, it is also not, primarily, a work of theory. It does provide useful tools from a variety of sources—including the work of some distinguished philosophers and intellectuals—but it does not seek to answer esoteric questions such as "what is virtue?" Third, this book is not a religious work. It does not take a partisan or sectarian position on theological matters, though it does deal with conflicts individual accountants may face when their religious beliefs are at stake in their professional lives (see Chapter 7).

Any reader of this book is entitled to ask, "Why work on ethical problems? What good will it do me?" A fuller answer to these questions will be apparent after reading the book. But some tentative responses are in order. Pursuing ethics in accounting can lead to clearer thinking. As a highly technical profession—one that demands the mastery of new knowledge and new skills—accounting is most absorbing. Rarely is there an opportunity to step back and to ask, "What are we doing and why are we doing it?" *Accounting ethics* is an invitation to scrutinize both one's personal values and the values embodied in one's professional activities.

In addition, working on accounting ethics gives a context to professional activity that is not usually encountered. Concerns about business in general, about social values in a rapidly changing society, and about the nature of accounting's reputation are raised in this book. New and emerging professional dilemmas—for example, the role of women in accounting—are discussed (see Chapter 9). Accounting is inherently connected to all sorts of public activity; the implications of these connections are raised in this book.

The structure of *Accounting Ethics* is as follows. After an introduction to several of the fundamental systems of ethical analysis and reasoning (Chapter 1), we look at the special situations in which professionals find themselves when moral dilemmas arise (Chapter 2). Accountants are pledged to a very fundamental principle, independence; the implications of this demand are discussed (Chapter 3). When serious problems are encountered in one's professional activities, the question of whether or not to "blow the whistle" is often presented (Chapter 4). Interpersonal possibilities, and attendant problems, are evaluated, with special attention to the growing phenomenon of mentoring (Chapter 5). Conflicts between legal obligations—in civil and criminal settings—and the behavior of accountants are analyzed (Chapter 6). Problems of personal conscience and professional mandates are raised and discussed (Chapter 7); an assessment of relationships among members of the professional community is presented (Chapter 8). New questions about the role of gender difference and discrimination are pursued (Chapter 9). Finally, issues about the profession's responsibility to society, per se, are raised (Chapter 10).

This book is practical. Each chapter describes and scrutinizes real-life situations. At the end of each chapter we append cases for the reader. We encourage doing accounting ethics—not by so-called experts but by practicing professionals and students. So we give you hard cases, with appropriate though not exhaustive questions, and ask you to get to work. A selective set of references is included at the end of the book.

NOTES

1. "The Case of the Singing CPA," *Newsweek*, July 17, 1989, p. 41.
2. W. Michael Hoffman, "The Cost of a Corporate Conscience," *Business and Society Review* 69 (Spring 1989), pp. 46–47.
3. Ibid., p. 47.
4. Peter Singer, *Practical Ethics* (Cambridge: Cambridge University Press, 1979), p. 1.

1

GETTING STARTED: ETHICAL SYSTEMS

- Ms. Jones has been with the firm for three years, yet she still receives few audit assignments of importance. The partner in charge, Mr. Roberts, says, "She still has a long way to go. These gals need more seasoning than the rest of us." Do you accept this explanation, or do you want to challenge it?
- Two conflicting interpretations of an important "item" in the annual report for Christmas Corporation are possible. One seems to be more "benign" than the other—it shows the company to be benevolent and socially useful. Yet it is not completely "accurate" to your way of thinking. As an internal auditor for the company, should you comment upon this item to the independent auditor?
- You are asked to participate in a consulting assignment for the ACME Cigarette Company, which is about to expand its foreign production. You are vehemently anti-smoking, believing it to be a major health hazard. You are especially concerned about the exporting of cigarettes and the advertising being done in Third World countries. Should you ask to be removed from the team undertaking this job? Should you raise this "social responsibility" issue higher up in the firm?

These scenes—and many more like them—are encountered in the everyday practice of accounting. Ethical dilemmas often involve uncertainty and, when rights and duties are in conflict, it is difficult to find guidance. We believe that honest, open, collaborative discussion of ethical issues in accounting is one way of dealing with such troubling problems.

Ethics is receiving wide-ranging discussion in today's popular press as well as in accounting literature. Many accountants find themselves perplexed by these arguments because they have not been exposed to a practical method of dealing with ethical dilemmas. No formal training and few opportunities in everyday working life have been provided for accountants on a sustained basis. Most accountants are very practical. They therefore resist ethical discussions that they perceive to be either moralizing in tone or abstract and philosophical in content.

Our purpose is not to present a philosophical treatise on ethics. Such discussions are widely available elsewhere. Neither do we intend to lecture the reader upon what moral values she should hold. We presume that our readers are people who already possess or aspire to high moral standards. Otherwise why would the topic of accounting ethics be of interest to them?

We shall present a useful, clear systems approach to ethics in accountancy. Accountants already know that the best way to evaluate the integrity of the financial information being communicated, both within the organization and to parties outside of it, is to understand and evaluate the accounting system used to convey this information. A parallel may be found in the realm of ethics. To understand an ethical dilemma and to analyze the potential resolution of a specific problem, one should seek to evaluate the strength of the particular ethical system in use.

This approach is equally valid on the individual, small group, and organizational level. We shall therefore begin with a brief description of the ethical systems you will find in today's business world as well as in society in general. These ethical systems will lay a foundation upon which we may build a deeper understanding of many of the ethical issues facing the modern accountant.

THE TWO FUNDAMENTAL SYSTEMS

Two ethical systems in particular have dominated the way that humankind thinks about ethics. We shall use these two systems for the most part in our ethical discussion (see Figure 1.1). Before we proceed with systematic treatments of ethical issues we shall briefly introduce these systems to you.

Utilitarianism

Balance is a concept close to the heart of every accountant. One of the first things we learn is to balance assets against liabilities and owners' equities. Utilitarianism can be best understood as a system of ethical balance. Here the desire is to find the balance of good consequences as opposed to bad consequences.

Figure 1.1
Utilitarian and Deontological Frameworks: Approaches to Ethical Decision Making

1. Utilitarianism: the promotion of the best long-term interest of everyone concerned should be the moral standard. Utilitarians look to consequences of acts for moral justification. They attempt to maximize good (or pleasure, or right) over harm (or evil, or wrong). Utilitarianism claims that rights and duties have no independent standing; that they derive from the goal of maximizing the overall good.

2. Deontology (from Greek: Duty): an action's or rule's consequences are not the only criteria for determining the morality of an action. Deontologists look to the features of the act itself, without regard for the consequences. They emphasize maxims, rules, principles (e.g., that promises must be kept). Morals, insist the deontologists, are based upon fundamental principles and not upon mere results.

* * * * *

UTILITARIANISM
(Consequences, Results)

BASIC: 1. Goal (e.g., maximize happiness)

DERIVATIVE: 2. Rights ← → 3. Duties

DEONTOLOGY
(Duties, Rules, Maxims)

BASIC: 1. Duties

DERIVATIVE: 2. Rights

SUBORDINATE: 3. Goals

4. Rights ← → 5. Duties

The utilitarian perspective about ethics claims that we should take those actions that lead to the greatest balance of good versus bad consequences. A dramatic illustration can serve to clarify the meaning here. Suppose that the year is 1942. You are a citizen of Frankfurt, Germany, and an active member of your church. The elders of the church have determined that the Nazi practice of incarcerating and executing people simply because they are Jewish is morally reprehensible. Therefore, the church is hiding a group of Jewish children in the basement.

One night there is a knock at the door of the church. When you open the door you find an officer in the Nazi S.S. standing there. He greets you and explains that his mission is to track down Jews for shipment to Dachau. He asks, "Are there any Jews in there?" Assuming that you think the officer will believe your answer, what is your reply?

Most people in today's society reply in this role-play situation that they would deny there are Jews in the church. Yet they do so with some squeamishness. Why do we find this so? The reason lies in the fact that most people use a utilitarian ethical system to solve this ethical dilemma.

Let's examine how this system works in this situation. When confronted with the question, the utilitarian moral agent will seek to weigh the probable consequences of the possible courses of action against each other and then choose the course of action that has the greatest amount of good (or least amount of bad) consequences.

In this case the consequences of telling a lie—or at least shading the truth—appear to be that innocent human life will be spared. Against this the agent weighs the fact that a lie itself is presumably "wrong." Most people weigh the good consequences of saving the Jewish children more heavily in this case and thus respond that they would lie to the S.S. officer.

Utilitarianism manifests itself in two major forms. The stronger of the two is so-called act-utilitarianism. Under this system, the moral agent considers the consequences of only the action under consideration. The second system is called rule-utilitarianism. Here the moral agent considers a set of rules by which life should be lived. The basis of accepting or rejecting a rule is whether the consequences of everyone following the rule will result in the maximum probable good consequences.

Rule-utilitarianism may be regarded as a weaker form of utilitarianism than act-utilitarianism. A rule-utilitarian, when confronted with a situation in which he believes that abiding by the rule will not in the present case be most beneficial, will simply modify the rule. Ultimately, this would end logically in one rule, "maximize probable benefit," which is the position of the act-utilitarian. Had the person who answered the door in our Nazi example been a rule-utilitarian, a possible rule might have been "do not lie." Yet the rule could have been modified to "do not lie except to save innocent human life."

Most accountants are already familiar with a system that acts very much like utilitarianism: cost/benefit analysis. In the cost/benefit system the accountant/manager attempts to balance the probable costs of taking a particular course of action with the probable benefits to be derived. Most accountants realize that cost/benefit analysis becomes more and more sticky as the analysis moves away from measurability in terms of dollars. Measurement of benefits has been particularly problematic.

Nevertheless, cost/benefit analysis appeared prominently in the accounting literature in arguments about an ethical issue of interest to the profession: social responsibility accounting. Writers on this subject have attempted to balance the costs of companies reporting on their adherence to social responsibility with the costs of not doing so. We will have a more thorough discussion of social responsibility accounting in Chapter 10.

Critics of utilitarianism have pointed out many flaws. One is the apparent ability of utilitarianism to justify the imposition of great suffering on a few people as long as benefit is derived by many people. A second, more practical criticism centers around the difficulty of defining the probable benefits, called "utility," and somehow summing them. Great disagreement may be generated over which consequences are in fact "good," which consequences should receive greater or lesser weight, and what probability should be assigned to different future consequences. Modern critics of utilitarianism also note that ultimately utilitarianism must seek non-utilitarian answers on assigning boundaries and values around the measurement of activities and values associated with the calculation of utilitarian systems. All these matters serve to cause what appears to be an exceptionally practical system to become less and less practical.[1]

Deontologism

The second major system of ethics found in modern society is deontologism. The term stems from the Greek word *deon*, which means duty. In contrast with the utilitarian ethical system, deontologism holds that right action is independent of consequences. Deontological theories focus instead upon the correctness of the action itself. The assumption is that there are duties, rules, and principles that are inherently valuable and should never be violated. We respect the law, for example, because it is correct to do so, not because it smooths the way in which the courts or the police operate. Deontological theory is anti-utilitarian: it states that an action is morally correct if it is rooted in a true moral principle. A moral person has a duty to take the right action regardless of consequences.

While much deontologism comes from religious directive, for example, "thou shalt not kill" as a strict moral rule, strong philosophical support also exists. The premier deontologist was Immanuel Kant (1724–1804), who prescribed a just society that could come about only if all persons based moral decisions upon the "categorical imperative":

One should take that action that he or she would wish everyone to take in all circumstances, irrespective of the consequences of the single, individual action. For example, Kant believed the moral choice to be truth telling irrespective of the consequences, since if no one told the truth we would have chaos in society because communication would be meaningless. To the categorical imperative Kant added the "practical imperative," that in considering actions one must treat all persons, including oneself, as an end and never as a means.[2]

Many people who have reflectively considered Kant's suggestions have found his categorical imperative too rigid. More flexibility was given to deontological ethics by W. D. Ross, a premier Kantian scholar who wrote during the middle of this century. Ross identified seven prima facie duties that he believed to be intuitive. They are fidelity, reparation, gratitude, justice, beneficence, self-improvement, and nonmaleficence. Ross contended that adherence to these duties was the preferred moral course of action irrespective of the consequences foreseen in a particular circumstance.[3]

Brief consideration should be given to the most prominent modern major ethicist who has written from the deontological view, John Rawls. He calls his theory "justice as fairness." The viewpoint is complex but may briefly be described as stepping away from a situation mentally and pretending that you will predetermine right action in a particular society without knowing what role you would have in that society. Without benefit of knowing one's role in society, an ethical agent can make a judgment about justice that is fair, since it is untainted by the self-interest of that agent.[4]

Perhaps another illustration can point out the use of deontological ethics. Suppose you are vacationing in a beautiful Central American country and are taking a drive on a solitary and scenic mountain road. Suddenly you round a hairpin curve and are confronted with a rather unpleasant situation. A platoon of men and women in khaki uniforms is leading nine bound and blindfolded Indians toward a wall where a firing squad awaits.

Appalled, you jump out of the car, find the officer in charge, and ask for an explanation. She is quite gregarious and cheerfully explains that the Indians have just been captured and that they will momentarily be executed. To your inquiry on the crime they have committed she states, "They have committed no crime per se. They are poor and of no value to our society, so we are going to rid the province of them."

When you express outrage at this, the lieutenant says she is greatly honored to have an American in her province. Therefore, she has decided to grant amnesty to eight of the Indians. She hands a pistol to you and says you are to choose which of the Indians will be freed by shooting the one who must die. What action would you take and why?

As in the hypothetical case of the Nazis at the door, most people respond to this situation in the same way. In this case the response is an indication that they would refuse to accept the offer of the Central American lieutenant. Notice that this decision runs entirely against an ethical system based upon utilitarianism. The clear-headed utilitarian would note that the option of shooting one person appears to have less evil consequences than the other apparent options—refusing to take part, shooting the lieutenant, and so forth—all of which would result in the death of at least nine people as opposed to one.

So why do most of us choose an option that results in more bad consequences? For the answer we must turn to a deontological perspective. Most of us believe deeply that it is simply wrong to kill without justification or, to put it in deontological terms, we have a duty not to kill. This belief will come from different foundations for different people. Ross, for example, would call this the duty of nonmaleficence. No matter where the belief comes from, the fact remains that the vast majority of us hold the view that taking innocent human life is wrong per se. We therefore, because of duty, believe that we would take a course of action leading to a greater degree of bad consequences in the hypothetical situation involving the helpless Central American Indians.

The deontological perspective has its share of critics. With respect to Kant's ideas, moralists have pointed out that both the categorical imperative and the practical imperative can clash with human welfare and even prescribe actions that lead to human suffering. For example, the strict Kantian would tell the truth to the Nazi S.S. officer, reasoning that the action of telling a lie is wrong per se and that any perceived consequences should not be considered. Ross's point of view is less vulnerable to this criticism but is subject to the weakness of answering the question of the source of the prima facie duties and whether there might be more prima facie duties. In other words, the moral agent might reasonably ask why she should accept Ross's duties as her own. The Rawls system suffers from the lack of reality involved in the role-playing requirement.

PERSPECTIVES ON THE MAJOR SYSTEMS

Utilitarianism and deontologism together constitute the two major ethical systems with which most modern ethics deals. Usually they are presented in contrast to one another. Figure 1.1 depicts this contrast between the two systems. Note the emphasis upon the consequences of action under utilitarianism. Once the moral agent has settled upon the goal or what is to be maximized, then ethical questions are settled in terms of meeting the goal. This is true both with respect to making decisions about future courses of action and about evaluating actions taken in the past with respect to their ethical propriety.

On the other hand, the deontological view concentrates upon the action itself. The thrust for the moral agent is to do his duty. Out of this comes rights for both himself and for others in society. Finally, the goal of a more ethical society is reached because in the ideal everyone is doing his duty.

The focus upon the differences between the two systems often obscures the fact that much of the time the two views will lead to the same decision with respect to an ethical issue. Let's consider a modern day phenomenon, sexual abuse of children, and discover how the seemingly opposite views of ethics can and do arrive at the same conclusion with respect to the ethics involved.

First we will propose a utilitarian view of the issue. The consequences of child abuse are extremely negative with respect to the child involved, both emotionally and physically. Almost any clear-thinking utilitarian would weigh these negative consequences much more heavily than the perceived pleasure the child abuser gets or against any issue of freedom from interference raised by a child abuse advocate. The result would be condemnation of child abuse.

Coming from an opposite point of view, any and all deontological systems with which we are familiar would condemn child abuse based upon the action itself being wrong. The Kantian perspective would stress the practical imperative as the reason the practice should not be permitted. Ross's system would look to non-maleficence, and Rawls would point out that no one would want to risk being the object of child abuse in a justice/fairness context.

Both utilitarianism and deontologism may be criticized in that neither seems to by itself describe the "ethics" found in today's society. Perhaps this may be explained by the fact that most of us are not ethical theorists, and we therefore borrow portions of our ethical responses from both major systems. Another possibility is that another system may better describe the reality of ethics. We will briefly describe a modern ethical theory that attempts to improve upon the way we practice ethics in our society.

ETHICAL REALISM

Some recent ethicists have suggested an ethical system, called ethical realism, that resolves the conflicts between utilitarian and deontological ethics. Ethical realism begins with the premise that moral concepts possess truth status. The theory specifically rejects the notion of empiricism—that is, in order to discover ethical truth, we must discover it by means of scientific method or experience. Ethical realists point out that their doctrine does not deny truth status to science; rather it says truth status in science and truth status in ethics are different matters. No contradiction need exist between science and ethics, nor is either necessarily considered a superior mode of thought. Each simply exists in its own realm.

This separation of ethics from science means that we need not rely upon a scientific method to discover what is right and what is wrong. Yet, if we cannot discover ethical truth from experience and experimentation, where might it be found? This is important to us because if, for instance, we are to conclude that some past deed was "good" or that some proposed course of action is "right," it is not enough for us to know that we ourselves are psychologically disposed to approve of the deed, or that the proposed course seems right to us. Rather, we must have reasons for thinking that the act was worthy of approval or that the course of action is worthy of selection.

The question remains: If we cannot discover ethical truth from empirical investigation or from our own psychological feelings, where is it to be found? The answer under ethical realism is that we look to so-called accepted intellectual authority relations that exist within the communities that we form. Sociologists tell us that we form communities in the first place by recognizing that it is to our benefit to renounce our claims and alter our aims where they conflict with other community members. Among the claims that we are willing to renounce and aims that we are willing to alter are ethical principles. Anyone wishing to be accepted as ethical but unwilling to do this is faced with the choice of working for change within the community or seeking another community with different intellectual authorities.

Thus intellectual authorities set ethical principles and appeal to a principle in ethical discussions. Such an appeal may be compared with an appeal to a scientific law in a scientific discussion. This is an evolutionary process. As all scientific laws are not equally well established, neither are ethical principles. In fact, within any moral community, one would expect to find ironclad ethical values as well as a developing moral code.

Let's explore whether ethical realism seems to "fit" what we observe experientially as accounting professionals. We find in accounting a strong sense of community. This is most obvious in the CPA profession but is becoming increasingly apparent in other sectors of the accounting profession as well. The notion that a profession is a community is a well-established principle among sociologists.

What about so-called "intellectual authorities"; where might we discover them in our accounting community? These are the leaders in our profession, the big guns. Each of us can name the national leaders in the profession. They are the managing partners of large firms, the heads of professional bodies, the members of standard-setting boards. In short, they are the men and women who have risen up through the ranks to positions of respect. As we can see, if we accept ethical realism as a valid doctrine for the application of moral concepts, the transition to ethics in accounting is a natural one.

Ethical change occurs in this system for the most part because leaders in the profession change their attitude toward an ethical principle. To state this formally, the leadership has an ethical insight. We have observed this happening in our profession with the change in attitudes about advertising and solicitation. At first, it may appear that advertising was forced upon the profession because the courts ruled that the profession could no longer prohibit it.

However, more careful consideration leads us to believe that there is more here than a change in the law. Suppose that the courts ruled that the profession no longer could exercise any type of control in matters where members were guilty of fraud. Would we expect accountants to rush headlong into the practice of dipping into company tills? Of course not! The reason is that we as professional accountants regard such a practice as unethical irrespective of the courts' view on the matter.

It is quite apparent that professional accountants do not view advertising and solicitation in the same light as embezzlement. Yet, for years we were told that the former practices were "unethical." We have here an example of an ethical insight. We would probably find that the professional leadership today believes advertising and solicitation were not unethical in the first place. That is, we as a profession were mistaken in our former belief.[5]

RELIGION: THE FINAL TABOO

Religion is a topic that is not found in most of the literature on accounting and business ethics. For some reason many of us regard religion as a deeply personal topic that we desire to keep separate from our professional lives. Yet when the subject is ethics, we should recognize that for a large segment of our society the religious and the ethical are so closely entwined that to ignore the former is to distort the latter. Dynamic ethical agents are simply unable to completely compartmentalize their lives.

For one whose ethical foundation is religion, the roots are either overtly or subliminally established in theology. Traditionally, theology has claimed to take its ultimate authority, indeed its fundamental validity, from "divine revelation." By this we mean that certain truths are not discernible by the unaided human mind but rather are known because God made them known in a special way. The religious background of the vast majority of the people in the United States is either Jewish, Catholic, or Protestant. We shall therefore find ethical principles that are rooted in religion in one of these three traditions for the most part.

The theology of these traditions is not itself uniform, but may be divided into conservative and liberal. Conservative theology finds divine revelation primarily in the Bible. For the Jew this consists of the Old Testament plus teachings of the great rabbis throughout the ages. For the Catholic the entire Bible is authoritative and the Catholic Church is seen as the only accurate interpreter of this divine revelation. The Protestant claims the Bible alone has the divine revelation and leaves it to the reader to interpret.

Liberal theology, in all three traditions, now tends to abandon the classical idea of divine revelation and makes religion essentially a dimension of human experience. Theology becomes a reflection on that experience and thus has no reference point outside that world of experience. Even within the liberal and conservative spectrums, vast differences may be found both in theology and, more importantly for our purposes, in ethical principle.

We should always consider the religious aspect when confronted with ethical dilemmas. Our own religious beliefs may be coming into play in ethical decision making. Even if this is not the case, the chances are great that we are constantly dealing with people whose religious views have an impact upon the ethical dynamic. We are not necessarily recommending advocacy of religion as much as awareness of the impact that religion can have in everyday practical ethics.

THE SYSTEMS VIEW

We have introduced two fundamental ethical systems and have kept them strictly segregated. In the "real world" we find that only the most dedicated philosopher is strictly wedded to a single ethical system. Most people, even when aware of the different kinds of ethics, blend the various systems in one form or another when they are confronted with an ethical decision. We do not propose to become advocates of one system over another. Rather we will look at ethical issues of interest to accountants from several viewpoints in order to heighten awareness and to enable the formation of intelligent bases for ethical judgments.

We have seen that ethics and accounting at least have one thing in common: there are different systems and each can give different information. The astute accountant understands many accounting systems and is able to use them both to gather information and to evaluate the validity and the quality of the information used to make financial decisions. The same should be true for the accountant whose questions are ethical rather than financial. The greater the awareness and understanding of the ethical system in use by oneself or another, the better each of us can evaluate the validity and quality of the ethical decision.

HARD CHOICES: DECISION MAKING IN VALUE-CONFLICT SITUATIONS

Most important cases in which there are ethical (and legal) issues are hard to "solve." Weighing wrong and right, reasoning clearly, testing potential solutions, looking for guidance to both principles and consequences—these activities are the essence of decision making.

Throughout this book we will present cases for your use in considering ethical issues more fully. No one is attempting to force you to take a particular position on a specific case. Rather, we ask you to examine a case carefully, understand its facts, look for the nuances, and then choose a justifiable analysis in order to enhance professional responsibility.

The following steps form a basis for responsible decision making.

1. Describe all the relevant facts in the case. Be certain to note any assumptions not directly presented in the case.
2. Describe the ethical and legal perspectives and responsibilities of the parties. Try to distinguish between legal and ethical responsibilities. Take note of potential value conflicts among participants in the case.
3. State the principal value conflicts in the case.
4. Determine possible courses of action. Note both short- and long-term consequences. Describe the principles affirmed or abridged in projected courses of action. Distinguish utilitarian (consequences)

from deontological (principles) justifications in each case. Would ethical realism as it exists in the accounting profession assist in resolving the dilemma?

5. Choose and defend a decision. State why one value (or set of values) was chosen over another in the case. Discuss the result of such a choice for participants in the case, for the accounting profession, and for society in general.

SUMMARY

As professional people increasingly under public scrutiny, accountants find themselves exposed to complex ethical issues. This book examines many ethical issues with which accountants struggle and points to ethical systems as tools that can be used to solve ethical dilemmas. By understanding the rational methods by which ethical issues may be examined, the professional accountant is better prepared to cope with complex ethical situations that are likely to arise in the professional working environment.

CASE STUDIES

1-1: EQUAL JUSTICE AND EQUAL TREATMENT

Having spearheaded the women's cause on behalf of equal pay for jobs of equal value, Betty Steinfried was elated when the board decided to readjust salaries in the light of that principle. Its decision was clearly important in the sense that Ms. Steinfried and other women employed by the crafts firm would receive pay equivalent to males doing comparable jobs. But in a larger sense it constituted an admission of guilt on the part of the board, acknowledgment of a history blemished with sexual discrimination.

In the euphoria that followed the board's decision, neither Ms. Steinfried nor any of the other campaign activists thought much about the implications of such an implied admission of female exploitation. But some weeks later, Jim Workout, a sales dispatcher, half jokingly suggested to Ms. Steinfried over lunch that she shouldn't stop with equal pay *now*. Ms. Steinfried asked Jim what he meant.

"Back pay," Jim said without hesitation. "If they're readjusting salaries for women," he explained, "they obviously know that salaries are out of line, and have been for some time." Then he asked her pointedly, "How long you been here, Betty?" Eleven years, she told him. "If those statistics you folks were passing around last month are accurate," Jim said, "then I'd say you've been losing about $500 a year or $5,500 over eleven." Then he added with a laugh, "Not counting interest, of course."

"Why not?" Ms. Steinfried thought. Why shouldn't she and other women who'd suffered past inequities be reimbursed?

That night Ms. Steinfried called a few of the other women and suggested that they press the board for back pay. Some said they were satisfied and didn't think they should force the issue. Others thought the firm had been fair in readjusting the salary schedule, and they were willing to let bygones be bygones. Still others thought that any further efforts might, in fact, roll back the board's favorable decision. Yet, there was a nucleus that agreed with Ms. Steinfried that workers who had been unfairly treated in the past ought to receive compensation. They decided, however, that since their ranks were divided, they shouldn't wage as intense an in-house campaign as previously, but take the issue directly to the board while it might still be inhaling deeply the fresh air of social responsibility.

The following Wednesday, Ms. Steinfried and four other women presented their case to the board, intentionally giving the impression that they enjoyed as much support from other workers as they had the last time they appeared before it. Although this wasn't true, Ms. Steinfried suggested it as an effective strategic ploy.

Ms. Steinfried's presentation had hardly ended when board members began making their feelings known about her proposal. One called it "industrial blackmail." "No sooner do we try to right an injustice," he said testily, "than you take our good faith and threaten to beat us over the head with it unless we comply with your request."

Another member just as vigorously argued that the current board couldn't be held accountable for the actions, policies, and decisions of previous boards. "Sure," he said, "we're empowered to alter policies as we see fit, as new conditions chart new directions. And we've done that. But to expect us to bear the full financial liability of decisions we never made is totally unrealistic—and unfair."

Still another member wondered where it would all end. "If we agree," he asked, "will you then suggest that we should track down all those women who ever worked for us, and provide them compensation?" Ms. Steinfried said no, but that the board should readjust retirement benefits for those affected.

At this point the board asked Ms. Steinfried if she had any idea of how much all of what she was proposing would cost the firm.

"Whatever it is, it's a small price to pay for righting wrong," she said firmly.

"But is it a small price to pay for severely damaging our profit picture?" one of the members asked. Then he added, "I needn't remind you that our profit outlook directly affects what we can offer our current employees in terms of salary and fringes. It directly affects our ability to revise our salary schedule." Finally, he asked Ms. Steinfried whether she'd be willing for the board to reduce everyone's current compensation in order for it to meet what she termed the board's "obligations to the past."

Despite its decided opposition to Ms. Steinfried's proposal, the board agreed to consider it and render a decision at its next meeting. As a final broadside, she hinted that if the board didn't comply with the committee's request, the committee was prepared to submit its demand to litigation.

Questions

1. If you were a board member, how would you vote? Why?
2. What moral values are involved in the case?
3. Do you think Ms. Steinfried was unfair in turning the board's implied admission of salary discrimination on the basis of sex against it? Why?
4. Do you think Ms. Steinfried was wrong in giving the board the impression that her proposal enjoyed broad support? Why?
5. If the board rejects the committee's request, do you think the committee ought to sue? Give reasons.

1-2: BUSINESS CONSEQUENCES OF SOCIETAL JUDGMENTS

Mr. Cloud has been employed in the accounting department of the Manna Company for seventeen years. Through his years of employment with Manna, Mr. Cloud has become familiar with all the company rules, including the rule stating that employees are terminated when found guilty of crimes.

Mr. Cloud committed the crime of "sexual imposition," which resulted in his being sentenced to two to three years in prison. His sentence was subsequently modified and he was placed on probation for three years and ordered to obtain psychotherapy.

While under indictment Mr. Cloud was continued as an employee by Manna, but was discharged when he pleaded guilty to the morals charge in exchange for the modified sentence.

Manna's company policy with respect to employees under indictment for crime is that the employee is innocent until proven guilty, but when found guilty, the employee is immediately discharged. This rule of employee conduct has been in effect for years and has been administered uniformly.

Manna's position is that modification of the sentence handed down by the court did not change Mr. Cloud's guilt. Manna feels that Mr. Cloud's crime of "sexual imposition" was a crime against society, and his guilt and conduct do not deserve consideration for employment with the organization.

As an aside, Mr. Cloud's son petitioned Manna to grant his father a leave of absence, rather than discharge him from the company, in consideration of the sentence modification. Manna stated that its policy did not allow for leaves of absence.

Questions

1. Did Manna unjustly discharge Mr. Cloud?
2. Is Mr. Cloud suffering double jeopardy (punished by both the courts and Manna for the same offense)?
3. What are some possible implications if Cloud's discharge is reversed?
4. What are some possible alternative solutions to this problem?
5. If Manna is a public accounting firm in which Mr. Cloud is a partner, does your answer change? Why or why not?

NOTES

1. See J.C.C. Smart and B. Williams, *Utilitarianism For and Against* (Cambridge, Eng.: Cambridge University Press, 1973) for a comprehensive discussion of the philosophical issues surrounding utilitarianism.
2. I. Kant, *Grounding for the Metaphysics of Morals*, trans. J. W. Ellington (Indianapolis, Ind.: Hackett, 1981).
3. W. D. Ross, *The Right and the Good* (Oxford, Eng.: Clarendon Press, 1930).
4. J. Rawls, *A Theory of Justice* (Cambridge, Mass.: Harvard University Press, 1971).
5. Readers interested in an in-depth discussion of ethical realism should consult S. Lovibond, *Realism and Imagination in Ethics* (Minneapolis: University of Minnesota Press, 1983).

2

PECULIARITIES OF PROFESSIONALISM: MORAL DILEMMAS

The designation "professional" is highly desired in our society and has been for centuries. People will even take courses of action that seem on the surface to be against their economic interest because they want to protect the privilege of being known as professional. An example would be the refusal to seek higher wages by participating in collective bargaining efforts for the primary reason that such an activity might appear unprofessional.

What is it about being professional that makes it so desirable? One pervasive aspect is the notion of community. Advocates of any profession attempt to set the professional apart from wider society. This is accomplished first through technical knowledge, then through an informal dynamics and language game that springs forth in the formative stages of professional development.

Professions are thus exclusive in nature. This exclusiveness makes the professional designation more valuable to its members. This value comes from both the obvious economic rewards available to successful professionals and from certain privileges granted by society to professions.

Professions rigidly guard entry. One who seeks admittance must demonstrate understanding of and acceptance of the profession's language game. The knowledge possessed by each profession is a source of power for that profession. Through their publications, meetings, examination syllabi, and other activities, various professional associations have historically played a role in defining and furthering the technical aspects of the profession, deciding who is competent to practice in that profession, and elaborating the discourse carried on by that particular profession.

THE NATURE OF PROFESSIONS

All professions have high standards for those licensed (or accredited) to practice them. Codes and standards, even oaths, are commonly encountered for doctors and lawyers, engineers and teachers, nurses and social workers. To be a professional is to achieve special status; the acquisition and maintenance of important skills is presumed for members of the profession. Above all, a professional achieves a new "identity" on entering a profession. A man or woman is no longer a bookkeeper, but a CPA, CMA, or CIA.

The marks of a professional are many. Doctors (most of the time) wear a white coat with a stethoscope hanging from the pocket; attorneys speak in Latin-sounding phrases (*res ipsa loquitur; mens rea*); engineers wear a hard hat *and* shirt with tie. Accountants are perhaps a little harder to tell from their non-professional business colleagues, but a conservative gray or navy business suit and audit bag at least provide evidence. The acronym after the name and membership in a professional society are other sure signs of special status.

Most authorities agree that a profession is characterized by four important elements:

- A specialized body of knowledge taught in a formal and certifiable manner
- A commitment to *social* purposes (good ones) that justify the profession's existence
- The capacity to regulate itself, often with the sanction of the law for those who violate acceptable norms of behavior
- Status and prestige of above-average ranking in society

To use accounting as an illustration of these four elements: accountants must study long (and hard), graduate from college with a minimum number of accounting and business hours, pass a lengthy and difficult examination, have character references, gather enough years of professional experience, and be able to perform specific tasks in a thorough and efficient manner in order to be specifically recognized. Moreover, accountants are increasingly required to satisfy continuing education requirements in order to keep their professional status.

Accountants do not claim professional privileges in order to maximize fame or fortune; rather, the profession's principal responsibility is neither to self nor to employer nor even to client, but rather to the public. Members of the profession who lie, cheat, steal, or behave in violation of standard practice are disciplined (at least in the preliminary stages) by the profession itself. Discipline may range from reprimand to expulsion.

Clearly, those who remain members of the profession in good standing achieve many benefits, including income and public recognition. These things are rewards for the achievement and maintenance of high standards. The esteem that derives from membership in an elite group makes professional status desirable.

Thus, a professional is not like other persons. He or she has a commitment to a way of life that is intellectually complex and demands constant updating of knowledge and skills. Public service, both direct and indirect, is presumed. Above the fray, behavior is scrutinized for its ethical dimensions. Accountants, like all professionals, make difficult judgments in which technical competence and moral values are intertwined. They confront moral dilemmas routinely. And they are held to the high standards of professional codes.

PROFESSIONALISM IN ACCOUNTING

By far the oldest and best developed professional group among accountants exists in public accounting. Amid much publicity and fanfare, the American Institute of Certified Public Accountants recently celebrated its one hundredth anniversary. Perhaps only doctors and lawyers can surpass certified public accountants in the claim to professionalism based upon history and longevity of public service. Evidence of the truth of this is found in the fact that the designation CPA is recognized by all fifty states and the federal government. Moreover, the AICPA and state societies of CPAs wield tremendous influence over the criteria for granting a CPA certificate.

It follows that the AICPA has the most fully developed standards of professional conduct found in accounting. Over the past two decades these standards have received considerable scrutiny from both the public and the courts. The AICPA has been astute in its degree of flexibility in maintaining control over standards while being willing to alter the standards themselves. The latest evidence of this is the *Code of Professional Conduct*, published in 1988.[1]

Other groups of accountants have recently taken actions designed to gain recognition as professionals. The two most prominent are the National Association of Accountants (NAA) and the Institute of Internal Auditors (IIA). Both groups have taken positive steps in recent years to clearly identify accountants as professional people.

Both groups have developed examinations and procedures to receive group certification. The National Association of Accountants has the certified management accountant. The Institute of Internal Auditors has the certified internal auditor. In addition, both groups have recently adopted codes of ethics.

CODES OF ETHICS

Clients served by professionals have no choice but to rely upon their doctors, lawyers, or accountants for expert advice. Professionals are assumed to have a command of a complicated and changing subject matter; that is why they have been hired. But this also means that clients are rarely able to evaluate the professional's competence. This is true in accounting as well as in the other professions. In accounting this is a more complex notion because of the issue of third parties. Chapter 4 discusses the third-party issue in greater depth. In any event, the professional expert is expected to serve the client's and not his own (or his firm's) best interests. Public confidence is based upon this foundation of trust.

Codes, and their enforcement, play a strong role in maintaining such public confidence. Accountants have a special reason to desire public support of their endeavors: businesses whose financial statements are audited pay for the accountant's services. Those who receive and rely upon published financial information must be confident of the independence of the professionals who conducted the audit. Can codes, by themselves, provide the means for a thorough enough scrutiny of professional responsibilities?

In the United States the accounting code of ethics with the longest history is that of the AICPA. Yet it is the most recent in its current form, having been revised and adopted on January 12, 1988. The new *Code of Professional Conduct's* principles cover the following broad areas: (1) Responsibilities; (2) The Public Interest; (3) Integrity; (4) Objectivity and Independence; (5) Due Care; (6) Scope and Nature of Services. The eleven rules in the code provide specificity to the principles.

The codes of ethics of the NAA and the IIA have a much shorter history than that of the AICPA. Both organizations adopted their codes during the 1980s. One concern frequently expressed about these codes is the seeming inability of the NAA and the IIA to enforce them. While a violation of the AICPA's code can lead to a prohibition from practice, the NAA and IIA do not have this power. Perhaps for this reason both codes are more general in nature and scope than the AICPA code.

The new codes of the NAA and the IIA come at a time when business in general is feeling pressure to have a code of ethics. Most accountants work in the business environment and those who do not interface with it. They therefore might find themselves confronted with two codes that could even be contradictory.

While codes of ethics in business and in professions have their use, they are not the "answer" to ethical issues. In fact, they can even augment an already existing problem, as Sissela Bok has pointed out:

> But codes of ethics function all too often as shields; their abstraction allows many to adhere to them while continuing their ordinary practices. In businesses as well as in those professions that have already developed codes, much more is needed. The codes must be but the starting point for a broad inquiry into the ethical quandaries encountered at work. Lay persons, and especially those affected by the professional practices, such as customers and patients [and clients and users], must be included in these efforts, and must sit on regulatory commissions. Methods of disciplining those who infringe the guidelines must be given teeth and enforced.[2]

Many accountants will bristle at the notion of lay persons regulating the profession as Bok suggests. There is a not so subtle warning in statements such as these; the proper response to criticism is to ascertain any truth in the criticism. Where fault is found, correct it. To ignore this advice is to risk the specter of having outsiders do it for the profession, perhaps in a heavy-handed way. We turn now to some of the current criticism being heard about our profession.

CRITICISM OF THE PROFESSION

Accountants are not without their critics with respect to their professional responsibilities. Public accounting is finding itself increasingly in the glare of publicity surrounding several issues of professional responsibility. The most prominently publicized are the responsibility of detecting fraud and the appropriateness of auditing the same firm for whom one has provided consulting services.

Public accountants are also being asked to re-examine their perspective of who receives their service. The Public Interest Section of the American Accounting Association in particular has criticized the profession for being too close to the clients at the expense of the readers and of identifying users exclusively as investors to the exclusion of labor, government, and other third parties.

Despite efforts at developing certification procedures and codes of ethics, those not in public practice have faced skepticism about their claims to professionalism. The primary problem is that the

National Association of Accountants and the Institute of Internal Auditors have precious few recourses available to enforce their codes of professional ethics. Moreover, the certificates they issue are not required for the practice of the profession. Many have questioned whether the necessary elements for professionalism are even present in these groups.

The struggle for professional recognition for accountants in either managerial accounting or in internal auditing still has a long way to go. On the other hand, the struggle in public accounting will be one of protecting the profession's already well established professional reputation. Ethical issues will be prominent in both of these arenas.

Even if we were completely persuaded that the standards of the profession—especially independence, objectivity, and integrity—are sufficient to guarantee conformity with code requirements, we would have many other ethical dilemmas to consider. Some are global (and apply to all professions); others are more specific (and deal with accountants as professionals).

Among the general questions all professionals must ask of themselves are the following:

- Do the standards of the profession exist for good reasons? Are these reasons clearly and sufficiently articulated?
- Is the present system of internal regulation fairly and consistently applied?
- Does "who you know" matter more than "what you know" when ethical judgments are made within the professional organization?
- Can the standards of the profession be understood by its membership, and by the public, in practical ways? Or are codes and guidelines unnecessarily jargon filled and complex?
- What ethical "blinders" are imposed upon insiders in a given profession? What is lost when critical distance lessens?

Accountants in particular will have these questions about professional responsibility and ethical conduct:

- To whom does the CPA owe duty? Are there conflicts between the duties owed to clients and the duties owed to third parties?
- Who are the third parties to whom the CPA owes duty? Are current reporting and auditing practices sufficient to meet duties owed to financial statement readers other than investors and owners?
- What professional responsibilities do CPAs have between and among one another? In light of recent court rulings with respect

to competition and the competitive environment that has followed, have these responsibilities been met?

- What exactly is the auditor's responsibility for the detection of fraud? Will the public accept a limited responsibility in the area? How can the profession better communicate with the public on this issue?
- For the accountant not in public practice, to whom are duties owed? How may conflicts between duties owed to third parties and desires of the employer be resolved?
- Are there any differences between the ethical duties of a professional accountant and a businessperson? If so, what are they and why do they exist?

CONFIDENTIALITY

Any trusting relationship entails the keeping of secrets. In medicine, law, and business, a relationship between professional and client (or patient) could never proceed unless a guarantee of protection of private information were either implied or explicit. Lawyers have been granted almost total privilege by the law. Physicians will not divulge information about a patient unless an authentic threat to public health (e.g., a communicable disease) is apparent. Members of the clergy also protect confidentiality as a means of freeing believers to confess without the fear of public notice.

What role should confidentiality play for accountants, especially since this profession has a strong ethical obligation to "tell the truth" to corporate officers, to shareholders, to governmental agencies, and (often) to society as a whole? A doctor must inform appropriate authorities if a gunshot wound is discovered. Must an accountant also abridge confidentiality if a clear and present danger is discovered?

First, we must distinguish two terms. The duty of *confidentiality* requires that information provided to the accountant shall not be disclosed without the specific consent of the client. For example, plans about future corporate activity must never be used for personal advantage: secrets may not be sold or bartered. A corollary of this duty is what courts call *privileged communication.* This concept states that a professional may not be called upon, in court or in another legally constituted body, to divulge confidential information. For example, a lawyer may not be compelled to testify about her client.

Accountants—and other professionals such as social workers, teachers, bankers, insurance agents, and journalists—do not usually enjoy this legal "privilege." But this does not mean that all information about client behavior must be divulged simply upon request, for example, from an investigating agency. The public statements of the major accounting organizations agree that the legal requirements to violate confidentiality must be respected. But this usually means that a "validly issued and enforceable subpoena or summons" must be on hand. Confidentiality is, if not a moral absolute for accountants, at least an idea that is taken very seriously.

There is another complicating factor regarding confidentiality in the profession. Can an accountant claim "privilege" when her own practice is being reviewed by a state board or regulatory agency? If this were possible, supervision and criticism of unethical or illegal practice would be at a standstill. Upcoming policy changes with respect to quality review will add increasingly sticky issues to the confidentiality issue. Nevertheless, for reasons of public policy as well as upholding professional standards (a clearly utilitarian balancing act), confidential information is often required to be released (in the most non-disclosing format possible) when such an investigation takes place.

Finally, we must note that confidentiality is justified on both utilitarian and deontological grounds. The client, the profession, and the public goodwill be served best, on balance, if full and fair disclosure of information is the norm. Such "truth-telling" activity is possible only if protected by law and ethical practice. This utilitarian validation of confidentiality is rooted in the prediction that all parties will be "happier" if secrets are kept. The deontological perspective on confidentiality has two aspects: (1) we have a duty to keep our promises (fidelity) and (2) we have a corollary duty to refrain from harm (non-maleficence), especially toward clients or dependents. Thus, if we state that information will not be divulged, we are morally obliged to protect such data.

The tricky item with regard to confidentiality arises when keeping secrets conflicts with other obligations. That is why dilemmas arise. That is why ethical analysis is required in hard cases.

ACCOUNTING COMMUNITY

So we see that what we call a profession is really a community. This community is not located at a physical place. Rather the location is defined by the activities in which the members engage and the values they hold. Members jealously defend the community by guarding the means to entry. Moreover, the profession decides and establishes criteria for continuing membership in this community. Among the values held by the community are moral and ethical standards. These standards are necessarily high so the community can be recognized by the larger society as "a profession."

It is quite easy to see that accounting meets the community standard of professionalism, including the high ethical standards. Accountants find themselves on a higher ethical plane than society in general for this reason. They must rise to meet the standards demanded by professional ethics. How well they do that ultimately determines whether they continue to hold society's coveted recognition as professionals.

CASE STUDIES

2-1: CONFIDENTIALITY AND INSIDE INFORMATION

Hope Noble has been employed as an auditor with Bradford Bakerson, a large regional CPA firm, for four years. Since last summer she has been dating Paul Cicotelli, who works as a manager with another CPA firm in the city. Their relationship had reached the serious stage and they had spoken about marriage on several occasions. The chief element preventing marriage is that they want to be more financially secure before they make that kind of commitment.

Tonight Paul has asked Hope out to dinner at an exclusive restaurant downtown. Over coffee and Benedictine after dinner Paul once again proposes marriage. The following conversation takes place.

Hope: Paul, you know I want to marry you, but we agreed to wait until we had ten thousand dollars in the bank.

Paul: Darling, our problems are over with respect to the financial concerns. I found out today from one of my clients, Kinder Toy, that they are going to announce tomorrow that they have landed an exclusive contract to sell their new line to the Toys-for-Tots chain.

Hope: So?

Paul: Don't you see? This should make Kinder Toy stock go up fifteen or twenty points, if not more. This is a major break. Anyway, I purchased five hundred shares from my broker today on margin.

Hope: But, Paul, isn't that an insider trading violation?

Paul: Oh, Hope, those laws are for the big players. I just want to make a few grand so we can get married. You are that important to me.

Questions

1. Is Hope confronted with a duty? If so, from where does it come? If not, why not?
2. Could Paul make an ethical case for his actions on utilitarian grounds? Defend your position.
3. Would your answer to question 1 change if Hope and Paul worked for the same firm?

2-2: A QUESTION OF LOYALTY

Cindy had been in her new position as controller of PGC Enterprise for about a month. She was beginning to feel she was finally getting her feet firmly planted and was enjoying the increased responsibility and opportunity that this job afforded her.

Cindy had come to PGC from its rival company, Everest and McKinley. The two companies were similar in many respects, since they were competitors in the same industry. They did differ in one key aspect. Everest and McKinley was a closely held partnership, and PGC was a public corporation.

Cindy had been with Everest and McKinley for eleven years. While there she had risen up the ranks to the position of assistant to the president for finance. Cindy was grateful to Everest and McKinley for all the things she had learned there, but when the position at PGC was offered to her it was too good to refuse.

On this particular afternoon, Cindy was attending an executive meeting at PGC with the president, John, and other high-level staff members. John was speculating that it looked as if Everest and McKinley had better control of their inventory costs than PGC. At least he felt that might be a reason Everest was able to get a price advantage in the Midwest market.

John: Say, Cindy, you were with Everest and McKinley quite a number of years. You must know something about their control system.

Cindy: Yes, I am somewhat familiar with it.

John: This presents a unique opportunity for us. You can tell us how that secretive outfit ticks.

Cindy: I'm sorry, but that is confidential information at Everest and McKinley.

John: Confidential information! Nonsense. We will tell anyone and everyone who wants to know that information about PGC.

Cindy: I know that, John; but Everest and McKinley has different standards.

John: Well, that's their problem. I'll tell you what. I would like a detailed report from you comparing as much as you remember about their system with the facts your staff can tell you about our system.

Cindy: I'm sorry, John. I wouldn't feel comfortable with that. I made a promise while I was with Everest and McKinley that I would never divulge any of their confidential information.

John: Then I suggest you adjust your "comfort zone." You work for PGC now and I expect your loyalty to be toward us. I would like to have that report by the close of business Monday.

Questions

1. Do a hard-choices workup for Cindy. Use ethical principles from utilitarian, deontological, and ethical realism models.
2. Assume the same facts except that the two firms are public accounting firms and the partner in charge is asking about confidential audit procedures. Would your response change? If so, how and why?
3. Again change the facts of the case. This time Everest and McKinley is a public accounting firm and PGC is a corporation. John wants confidential information about a rival that is a client of Everest and McKinley. Would your response change? If so, how and why?
4. Comment upon any differences—or lack thereof—that professionals may have that others do not, based upon your thinking about this case.

NOTES

1. American Institute of Certified Public Accountants, *Code of Professional Conduct*, as amended January 12, 1988.
2. S. Bok, *Lying: Moral Choice in Public and Private Life* (New York: Random House, 1978), p. 260.

3

INDEPENDENCE: ACCOUNTING AND INTEGRITY

Independence may be defined in a professional context as a state in which one is self-reliant and not easily influenced by others. Professionals rely upon their own expertise and judgment rather than opinions, biases, or emotions of other persons. Independence, as an ethical concept, is prominent in the accounting profession. Indeed, all professionals should be independent in that they should not subordinate their judgment to make a client happy.

Using some of the ethical concepts we have considered earlier, we may say that the professional should give no utilitarian weight to the happiness of the client. Some professionals, including accounting professionals, may succumb to this temptation. However, in the realm of public accounting, any consideration of the client's interests must be subordinated to a greater duty—the duty owed to third parties and to the public.

Let us consider the medical profession as an example of how utilitarian weight may be given to the well-being of the client as opposed to the happiness of the client. Suppose a patient comes to his doctor complaining of pain and requests a strong prescription painkiller by name. In the doctor's judgment the pain is illusory. Moreover, she knows that the painkiller requested by the patient is potentially addictive. In her judgment the risks of prescribing such a medication far outweigh any benefits to the patient. She therefore ought to refuse to grant the request even if she knows that this will displease the patient and that he may choose another doctor.

The sort of independence illustrated by this case means independence from the expressed will of the client. Because a key tenet of the whole notion of professionalism is that the professional has greater experience, ability, or familiarity with a certain area than a client, the professional should not subordinate professional judgment to client desire as a matter of ethical principle.

As in all professions, this aspect of independence is a well-established ethical norm in public accounting. In every engagement, including engagements of tax services and consulting, the CPA must refuse to subordinate her professional judgment to the judgment of the client. Like the doctor/patient relationship, a primary concern here is that the client will receive the best professional advice and service the professional CPA can provide.

A danger does exist in emphasizing independence. The danger is creeping paternalism. In medicine the fear is that the doctor will not hear the real story since she, as a professional, already has the "answer." The same danger can and does exist with respect to the CPA and her client. Ultimately some degree of mutual respect must exist between professional and client.

INDEPENDENCE AND PUBLIC ACCOUNTING

Independence is a more fundamental and pervasive concept in accounting than in the other professions. Indeed, former Chief Justice Burger stated that independence is a critical concept that sets CPAs apart from other professions.[1] This is true because the core mission of the CPA is as auditor, one who certifies the public reports that describe a corporation's financial status. This is the only exclusive function that the CPA performs for society.

In rendering an opinion the independent auditor assumes a public duty. Moreover, this public duty must transcend any employment relationship or other duty toward the client. The CPA has what Burger calls a "public watchdog" function that demands that the auditor subordinate responsibility toward the client in order to maintain complete fidelity to the public trust.

So important and ingrained is independence in the public accounting profession that it may be regarded as a cornerstone upon which much of the ethics peculiar to the profession is built. Note the radical change in focus when the accounting profession speaks of independence. The perceived peril in lack of independence is not to the client but to an outside third party. This third party may be any person who reads and relies upon the financial statements upon which the auditor has rendered an opinion.

We find that to serve the third party the auditor must take an unbiased viewpoint when he performs audit tests, evaluates the results of those tests, and then issues an audit report and opinion with respect to the financial statements. Traditionally accountants have viewed independence on three ethical planes. First, in order to take an unbiased viewpoint, an auditor must possess the virtues of honesty, objectivity, and responsibility. In other words, on this plane we are concerned with the character of the auditor. We may regard this as the highest form of independence.

At the second level independence refers to the relationship of the CPA and the client. Here independence means avoiding any relationship that would likely, even subconsciously, tend to impair the CPA's ability to take the unbiased viewpoint. The public accountant must avoid personal and business relationships with clients that could cause even the most well-meaning person to slip or compromise in professional judgment.

On the final level, independence means the CPA should avoid any relationship that might suggest to a reasonable observer that a conflict of interest exists. Even when the professional is completely satisfied that no relationship impairs her judgment as a professional, she has not gone far enough. She must concern herself with the jaundiced eye of the beholder. So, even is she is completely satisfied that she can render an impartial judgment or opinion for a client with whom she has a particular business relationship, the standards of the profession still might prohibit her from acting as independent auditor. In this respect we can compare the accounting profession with the legal profession, which demands of the judiciary that no appearance of impropriety exists.

We thus see that on two levels independence is a condition of the mind and character of the professional. On the third level the issue is not about the professional herself but the way others view her. The common expressions used in professional circles to describe these phenomena are independence in fact and independence in appearance.

INDEPENDENCE IN FACT

Independence in fact is one of the most elusive aspects of ethics in the accounting profession. Most public accountants are ready to assert that for the most part independence in fact is the norm in daily professional life. Yet they are at a loss to provide evidence for this assertion or even to explain why they believe it is true.

After all, it is difficult to discern the virtues necessary for independence in fact. Moreover, we have little basis to doubt the existence of independence in fact in a particular circumstance until the most dramatic of events, the audit failure, comes to light. An audit failure is said to occur when a CPA opines to third parties that a client's financial statements are fairly presented in accordance with generally accepted accounting principles when in fact they are not. Often the root of the audit failure is found to be a lack of independence in fact.

Some frequently cited examples of a lack of independence in fact include lacking objectivity and skepticism, accepting the work of management for something that normally requires independent verification, agreeing to a significant client-imposed restriction on the scope of the audit, or knowingly neglecting the critical evaluation of a significant client transaction. Failure to test the accounts receivable by independent confirmation would be a concrete example. Some people also believe incompetence is a manifestation of a lack of independence in fact. In each of these cases, the virtues required to render an unbiased opinion are missing. Independence is thus violated on its highest plane.

Another dimension of independence in fact originates in relationships with clients. The Securities and Exchange Commission, in Accounting Series Release 234, has tightened the restrictions here. "The application of an independent viewpoint is particularly important with respect to judgements exercised in the determination of appropriate principles and methods applied to the recording, classification and presentation of financial data. By their nature such judgements cannot subsequently be evaluated on an impartial and objective basis by the same accountant who made them."[2] In other words, the CPA cannot serve two masters: he cannot hold himself out to the public in a traditional auditor-client mode while at the same time serving that client as a controller, treasurer, or internal auditor. Neither can the CPA hold a direct financial or a material indirect financial interest in a client about whom he is rendering an opinion.

INDEPENDENCE IN APPEARANCE

Independence in fact exists when an auditor is actually able to maintain an unbiased attitude in the conduct of the audit. By contrast, independence in appearance refers to the interpretation or perception of others about the auditor's independence. Most of the value of the audit report stems from the independent status of the auditor. Therefore, if auditors are independent in fact, but readers of the financial statements or members of the public at large believe them to be advocates for the client, most of the value of the audit function would be lost. These users of financial information can have faith in an auditor's representations only when they are confident that the auditor has acted as an impartial judge.

The entire reason for a profession of public accounting rests upon the foundation of independence in appearance. Otherwise the audit function could be performed by internal auditors who work for the company. These men and women are honorable people who possess requisite virtue for performing audits. Moreover, organizational systems could be devised to protect them from management retaliation. It is therefore at least possible that they could be independent in fact.

Nevertheless, users would almost always have a lingering doubt about the statements' impartiality and freedom from bias. Readers might suspect that the auditors were really serving the best interests of the company for which they worked. In other words, the internal auditor would not appear independent. Hence her representations would not have value to the user. An analogous phenomenon may be found in our government, where an independent prosecutor is appointed when a federal official, especially one in the Justice Department, is accused of a crime.

Concern about lack of independence in fact not only lowers the value of a particular audit report but also can have an adverse effect on the profession. Certified public accounts are given special status in society—the status of "professional"—because of the perceived role that they play in that society. The role of the auditor is to give an unbiased opinion on reported financial information based upon professional judgment. If CPAs on the whole are not viewed as independent, the validity of the auditors' role in society is threatened. The very credibility of the profession, public accounting, depends ultimately upon society's perception about independence rather than the fact of independence.

AREAS OF CONCERN

Four areas in particular are significant with respect to independence in appearance: (1) the competition that now exists among audit firms; (2) the increasing role of management advisory services offered by auditors; (3) the large and growing size of audit firms; and (4) the length of time an audit firm has been filling the audit needs of a given client. Each of these areas has the potential of weakening public perception about certified public accountants' independence.

The competition we observe today among auditors was brought about because of action of the Federal Trade Commission and a Supreme Court decision.[3] Before these events CPAs kept themselves above the fray, so to speak. They seemed content with their existing client base and were constrained by the then existing code of ethics from doing much to change that base. This way of doing business, despite being declared illegal, at least gave the illusion of being "professional."

Today auditors conduct business in a more capitalistic fashion utilizing advertising, personal selling, and other advanced marketing techniques to capture as much of the audit market as they can. It is all perfectly legal and legitimate business activity, but somehow it does not seem as "professional." The lingering question in the mind of the outside observer is whether a professional might not be willing to sacrifice independence in order to gain business advantage in an unrestrained competitive environment. Notice that the primary problem here is the appearance rather than the fact of independence.

The role of CPAs as business consultants through their management advisory services creates a similar problem. This role of the auditor is admittedly an old one. Yet today it is increasingly important to the practice of public accounting because competition for audit clients has made audit service less profitable. Moreover, the profitability of these services has been followed by increased publicity concerning the activities of CPAs in the consulting area. This is compounded by the fact that CPA firms have expanded into more and more diverse areas of consulting.

The problem once again is how the public perceives all of this. Can a person play this increasingly important role as an advisor to clients on how to conduct their businesses and at the same time give an unbiased opinion about the reported financial information? The profession strongly defends the position that by keeping auditing and consulting activities separate, independence is in fact maintained. Perhaps this is true. Yet the very fact that the question is raised means that independence in appearance is threatened.

A third problem with respect to independence in appearance arises due to the sheer size of the firms in which many certified public accountants practice. Increasingly the profession is being dominated by huge, multinational firms known as the Big Six. Ethically, there is nothing wrong here. But to the public these large firms are beginning to look more and more like big business. Therefore, these firms must be especially careful to guard against perceptions of a lack of independence.

A final factor that can erode independence in appearance is the length of time a particular client is served by a single auditor. In many cases an auditor-client relationship has stretched across decades. As time passes the client and the firm are increasingly identified with one another in the public eye. Again, the danger here is in appearance. The organizations may seem to be too close in the eye of the beholder even if the strictest measure of independence in fact is maintained.

Problems of credibility in each of the above cases almost always arise outside the profession. Therefore accountants must be constantly aware of the perception issue, which can have an adverse impact upon auditing firms and the direct and indirect users of their services. The issue is rarely concerned with the validity of negative perceptions, but rather the *belief* that users and society hold with respect to objectivity and freedom from bias.

THE CODE OF ETHICS

Concern about the issues of both independence in fact and independence in appearance is clearly reflected in the current Code of Professional Conduct of the American Institute of Certified Public Accountants (AICPA). Currently this code of ethics consists of two sections—(1) the principles and (2) the rules. The principles are designed to provide a framework for the rules. In turn the rules are designed to govern the performance of professional services by members of the AICPA.

We first encounter the concept of independence as a principle. Article IV, Objectivity and Independence, states: "A member should maintain objectivity and be free of conflicts of interest in discharging professional responsibilities. A member in practice should be independent in fact and appearance where providing auditing and other attestation services."[4] Note that by making independence a principle, the AICPA formally raises independence to the level of a deontological construct of the profession.

Independence resembles a deontological principle rooted in one of Ross's prima facie duties: fidelity. By holding herself out as a certified public accountant, the auditor is making a faithful promise to the public when she signs an opinion on the client's financial statements. She is promising that her opinion is based upon her best professional judgment and is free from bias. In order to keep this promise she must maintain independence in fact.

With respect to its membership, the AICPA imposes stricter standards upon those who practice as public accountants. Those members must hold to the principle of independence in fact and to the principle of independence in appearance. Members who are not in public practice are required only to adhere to independence in fact. This recognizes that maintaining independence in appearance with one's employer is impossible.

The AICPA closely links independence with the auditor's ability to render an objective opinion based upon professional judgment. "Objectivity is a state of mind, a quality that lends value to a member's services. It is a distinguishing feature of the profession. The principle of objectivity imposes the obligation to be impartial, intellectually honest, and free from conflicts of interest. Independence precludes relationships that may appear to impair a member's objectivity in rendering attestation services."[5]

The AICPA rule on independence is a rather straightforward statement that a member in public practice shall be independent. The AICPA believes the appearance of independence is so important that it gives a rather lengthy interpretation of the rule on independence:

Independence shall be considered to be impaired if, for example, a member had any of the following transactions, interests, or relationships:

A. During the period of a professional engagement or at the time of expressing an opinion, a member or a member's firm

1. Had or was committed to acquire any direct or material indirect financial interest in the enterprise.

2. Was a trustee of any trust or executor or administrator of any estate if such trust or estate had or was committed to acquire any direct or material indirect financial interest of the enterprise.

3. Had any joint, closely held business investment with the enterprise or with any officer, director, or principal stockholders thereof that was material in relation to the member's net worth or the net worth of the member's firm.

4. Had any loan to or from the enterprise or any officer, director, or principal stockholder of the enterprise. This proscription does not apply to the following loans from a financial institution when made under normal lending procedures, terms, and requirements:

a. Loans obtained by a member or a member's firm that are not material in relation to the net worth of such borrower.

b. Home mortgages.

c. Other secured loans, except loans guaranteed by a member's firm which are otherwise unsecured.

B. During the period covered by the financial statements, during the period of the professional engagement, or at the time of expressing an opinion, a member or a member's firm

1. Was connected with the enterprise as a promoter, underwriter or voting trustee, as a director or officer, or in any capacity equivalent to that of a member of management or of an employee.

2. Was a trustee for any pension or profit-sharing trust of the enterprise.

The above examples are not intended to be all-inclusive.[6]

Financial Interest

Note the distinction made between direct and indirect financial interest. Direct financial interest refers to the ownership of stock in a client and applies to the CPA and members of his immediate family. Indirect financial interest occurs in two ways. One is where there is an intervening institution, such as when a CPA has interest in a mutual fund that in turn owns stock of the CPA's client. The other is when the ownership is by someone related to the CPA, but not in his immediate family, such as a grandparent.

The standard of materiality is applied only to indirect financial interest. Materiality, like beauty, exists in the eye of the beholder. This is quite appropriate for independence in appearance. Here materiality refers to the wealth of the CPA and to the amount of ownership. If a large portion of a CPA's personal wealth were invested in a mutual fund that in turn owned a large portion of that CPA's client, independence would be violated under the rules.

In the realm of financial interest, the AICPA holds that the rule on independence applies to all partners and shareholders for all clients of a particular CPA firm, not just the partner on the audit engagement. Non-partner CPAs who work for large auditing firms are not affected by the rule as long as they are not in the office doing the audit or involved in the audit in any other way. However, many of the large CPA firms hold their staff to a higher standard and do not permit anyone on the professional staff to own stock in any client of the firm.

Further Interpretations of the Rules

CPAs are prohibited from serving on the board of directors of a company, primarily because of independence in appearance considerations. The concern is that in these capacities the CPA is working too closely with the managers who make the decisions in a company. This proximity to the decision-making process could at least create the illusion that independence did not exist in the conduct of the audit. Exceptions to this rule are generally made when the partner of a CPA firm serves as an honorary member of a board of a charitable institution that the firm audits, so long as that partner does not participate in any management decisions.

Independence is generally considered lost when litigation arises between the CPA firm and the client. It does not seem reasonable to expect the professional to maintain objectivity in circumstances where she is either suing or being sued by the client. In cases where the CPA and the client are both being sued by a third party, independence is usually not deemed to have been impaired.

Sometimes a CPA is asked to perform bookkeeping services for the client. Is independence maintained if the same CPA conducts the audit? This role is allowed under strict guidelines where it is clear that the client assumes responsibility for the financial statements, that the CPA is not a client's employee or agent, and that generally accepted auditing standards are adhered to with respect to the sets of books that the CPA has maintained.

INDEPENDENCE AND MANAGEMENT ADVISORY SERVICES

Concern about the potential conflict between a public accounting firm's role as auditor and business consultant to the same client is an old one. Almost twenty-five years ago J. L. Carey and W. O. Doherty, in their book on ethics published by the AICPA, used two primary arguments to support the CPA's dual role. The first was that consulting fees were minor when compared with audit fees. Thus the CPA would be careful not to place the latter at risk. The second was a rejection of the notion that we should have two kinds of accountants—auditors and consultants.[7]

Today both arguments hold no validity. The fees collected for management advisory services (MAS) work are now more profitable for many firms than fees for audit services. At the same time, because of the complexity of the MAS work done by large public accounting firms, the functions of audit and MAS are clearly segregated in most instances. With these developments in the profession, the controversy about the propriety of the same firm doing MAS work and issuing an opinion on financial reports is again on the front burner.

The distinction between independence in fact and independence in appearance must be kept in mind. Some theoretical research conducted by A. Goldman and B. Barlev yielded some rather surprising conclusions with respect to independence in fact. These researchers argued that the greater amount of power a party in a relationship has, the greater that party's actual independence. Furthermore, they concluded that the higher the proportion of non-routine problems dealt with by a professional, the more power he wields vis-à-vis the client. Moreover, the higher the proportion of services the professional renders directly to the paying client, the more important are these services to the client. Hence, the power of the professional is greater and the professional's degree of independence is enhanced.[8]

The conclusions of these researchers fly in the face of both conventional wisdom about independence and the problem of independence in appearance. The former chief accountant of the Securities and Exchange Commission, John C. (Sandy) Burton, tends to verify these conclusions from his own experience. Burton notes that supposed conflicts between MAS work and audit services are seldom buttressed by empirical data of either a systematic or anecdotal nature. In fact, Burton's experience indicates that too little involvement by auditors in the affairs of clients creates more problems than too much involvement.[9]

We are left, then, with the independence in appearance problem facing the auditor. Here the perception in the eye of the beholder is the primary problem. Burton notes that it is critical to consider who the beholder is:

> The basic question to be resolved in dealing with an appearance criterion is whether appearance should be examined on the basis of that which would be perceived by an informed person with knowledge of the facts or by a person with no understanding of the audit process or the relationships that conventionally exist. Most reported surveys of the perceptions of independence indicated that the greater the degree of knowledge about the profession and auditing, the less concern there is about threats to independence emerging from the scope of services performed. On the other hand, those without information or background of this sort are inclined to perceive a problem.[10]

Thus we see that by its very nature independence creates a tension between fact and appearance. More MAS work may increase the CPAs independence in fact. Those with a high degree of understanding about auditing apparently appreciate this and are not concerned about conflicts of this sort. Yet, independence in appearance is a construct designed for the lay public, those who do not have a high degree of understanding about the audit process and independence in fact. It is for these people that the concept of independence in appearance was designed. Therefore the profession must take care to maintain the fact and the appearance of independence.

OTHER CURRENT ISSUES

One of the most troubling questions that may be asked about independence is whether a CPA may truly maintain independence in fact and appearance while accepting a fee from the client. Some critics have suggested that the solution to this dilemma is to have the government or some other public agency pay the auditor's fee.

Such suggestions have not met with great favor within the profession as a whole.

Opinion shopping is another troublesome area. It is sometimes alleged that when a company is displeased with the professional judgment of the independent auditor, management has the option of finding an auditor whose professional judgment is more to management's liking. This allegation, if true, would obviously tempt the independence of the first auditor in the event of a difference of opinion. Moreover, the independence of the second audit firm can also be impaired if they accept an engagement based upon an opinion they discussed and once involved in the engagement they find the facts and circumstances to be different than originally represented by management. The AICPA has taken steps in its official auditing standards to attempt to protect auditors from a loss of independence in these circumstances.

One movement that has enhanced the independence of the auditing firm is the formation of audit committees made up of members of the corporation's board of directors. Ideally, these board members are outside directors who are not part of the company's management. The duties and powers of audit committees vary from company to company, but their objective is primarily to protect the independence of the outside auditor.

Audit committees are a requirement for listing on the major stock exchanges and over-the-counter markets. In addition, the Securities and Exchange Commission strongly encourages them. Some concern has been expressed that audit committees might create an anti-competitive effect in public accounting, but recent research has failed to support this allegation.

CONCLUSION

Independence—the very foundation of the profession rests upon this concept. Debate about it will continue if the profession is to remain viable, for such debate is an indicator of ethical health. Accountants must continually seek to strengthen the ethics of independence. Perhaps the greatest danger to the profession lies in potential apathy toward independence. If the public and its representatives were ever to perceive that independence was a sham, the profession would likely be swept away like a sand castle before the tides.

CASE STUDIES

3-1: INDEPENDENCE IN FACT AND APPEARANCE

Brian Cox had started his wholesale hardware lumber company upon graduating from Lee and Grant College. The early years had been lean, and Brian was truly grateful for his wife, Barb, who had carried the family financially.

Barb worked for the multinational CPA firm, Longstreet, Early, and Stewart. Her position with LES was rather unusual in that Barb was not an accountant but a human resources specialist. Barb had been quite successful with the firm and currently was a senior manager on the verge of being promoted to principal.

Brian's business was located in Cincinnati while Barb worked in Dayton. LES had large offices in both cities. The couple currently lived in a suburb between the two cities so commuting time was minimized for both. Their business contacts with one another were nil.

On this particular day Brian was mulling over his company's need to make a change in accounting. The business had grown to the point where the small local practitioner could not give the services that Brian required. Therefore Brian was looking for a new outside auditor. After careful consideration Brian had determined that LES would be the best for his business.

When Brian casually mentioned his decision to Barb, she told him she did not think LES would accept the engagement once they realized that she and Brian were married. Brian thought that this was ridiculous. He reasoned that the fact Barb worked for LES had not entered into his decision and it should not enter into theirs. Besides, they were in different cities and Barb had nothing whatsoever to do with the auditing function. Brian became determined that he would convince the Cincinnati partners of LES to accept him as a client.

Questions

1. Suppose that you are the managing partner of the Cincinnati office of LES. Under what circumstances, if any, would you accept this engagement?
2. Prepare a brief position paper that could be used to explain your position to Brian.
3. Are there any differences between independence in fact and independence in appearance in this case? Explain briefly.

3-2: INDEPENDENCE AND MANAGEMENT ADVISORY SERVICES

Cotter Philpot is an audit partner with a large regional CPA firm, Berdine & Co. He is currently engaged in the audit of Seefeld Ltd., which manufactures a full line of flutes. A senior on the job has brought to Cotter's attention that a review of the cost accounting system has revealed an extremely large unfavorable material quantity variance. In Cotter's professional judgment this variance is so large that it is material. He therefore believes it should be placed on the income statement as a non-recurring item.

Just two years ago the management advisory services (MAS) department of Berdine & Co. had landed a sizable contract with Seefeld Ltd. to examine their cost accounting and control system. Based upon the recommendations made by the MAS department, Seefeld Ltd. implemented a major overhaul of its cost accounting and control system throughout the operation. In Cotter's opinion, this new system contained a major flaw that was directly responsible for the large unfavorable material quantity variance. Because of this, Cotter has elected to talk over the situation with the partner in charge of the office, Mary Blazewell, before speaking with the management of Seefeld Ltd.

Mary has also reviewed the working papers sent to her by Cotter and has concluded that the unfavorable materials quantity variance has been properly calculated. She has also consulted with the MAS department and has concluded that Cotter is right—the variance can be directly traced to the new cost accounting and control system implemented by Seefeld Ltd. upon the recommendation of Berdine & Co. She does not, however, agree with Cotter's judgment as to the accounting treatment of the variance.

During a conversation over lunch, Mary gives Cotter some of her thoughts. "You know, Cotter, this is the biggest blunder I have ever seen the MAS staff make. I hate to rub salt in the wound by making Seefeld Ltd. put that variance right on the income statement."

"I've talked with the theory experts at the head office and they told me this thing can be looked at two ways. Under standard cost theory your accounting treatment is correct. However, if we go with actual cost theory we can prorate that variance among several inventory accounts and cost of goods sold. That way it will wash out of the system."

"Cotter, things have been intense for Berdine & Co. since those three 'Big Six' firms moved into town. It's tough competing with them; we've already lost a couple of clients. The Seefeld Ltd. job is absolutely vital to us. They are our biggest client in this area."

I'm afraid I'm going to have to overrule you on this one, Cotter. The theory people tell me actual cost theory has as much, if not more, support than standard cost theory anyway."

Questions

1. Does the AICPA rule on independence come into play in this case? If so, how; if not, why not?
2. Can you support the concept of independence from a deontological perspective or from a utilitarian perspective?
3. Does the AICPA rule on integrity and objectivity apply to Cotter in this case?
4. If Cotter is a strict Kantian, what action do you believe he would take and how would he defend it? What if he were a strict act-utilitarian?

NOTES

1. *United States* v. *Arthur Young & Co. et al.*, 79 L.Ed. 2d 826–38 (1984).
2. Securities and Exchange Commission, *Accountants Qualifications, Interpretations and Guidelines*; Accounting Series Release No. 234. *Federal Register* 42, 246 (December 22, 1977), pp. 64304–309.
3. *Bates* v. *State Bar of Arizona*, 97 S. Ct. 2691, 45 U.S. Law Week 4895 (1977).
4. American Institute of Certified Public Accountants, *Code of Professional Conduct*, as amended January 12, 1988, p. 5.
5. Ibid., pp. 5–6.
6. Ibid., pp. 9–10.
7. J. L. Carey and W. O. Doherty, *Ethical Standards of the Accounting Profession* (New York: AICPA, 1966).
8. A. Goldman and B. Barlev, "The Auditor-Firm Conflict of Interests: Its Implications for Independence," *The Accounting Review*, October 1974.
9. John C. Burton, "A Critical Look at Professionalism and Scope of Services," *Journal of Accountancy*, April 1980.
10. Ibid., p. 51.

4

WHISTLE-BLOWING: PRINCIPLES IN PRACTICE

The ZAP Company is a major multinational corporation, one of the top fifty American organizations, and is heavily invested in high technology operations. The ZAP factory in Industrial City manufactures copper wiring. This older plant (built in 1939) flushes high concentrations of copper into the municipal sewerage system. Industrial City's sanitary district allows a minimal amount of effluent to be drained into the system, but ZAP is pouring twice the maximum amount into the sewers on a daily basis. Copper is a toxic substance for water animals but rarely for humans.

Joe Storms is a cost accountant working at the ZAP plant. In the course of his everyday activity, he learns about the violations of the city's regulations and becomes aware of the environmental dangers. He speaks to his immediate superiors; they ignore him. He makes an appointment to see the plant manager and tells him of his concerns. Mr. Clyde (the manager) tells Joe three things: (1) the plant will soon be sold to another company; (2) ZAP intends to build a new factory in the suburbs with state-of-the-art anti-pollution equipment; (3) no city inspector has ever given the present plant notice of any pollution from copper. He tells Joe: "This is no big deal. No people are harmed. Don't make waves. We'll be out of the city in less than two years."

Joe is very worried about his responsibility to his firm, to the stockholders, and to the public. He is also concerned about his own situation—no one likes a whistle-blower—and about what might happen to his family if he raises the issue further. And what about his own professional career? Furthermore, what are his responsibilities to the accounting profession? A few days after meeting with Mr. Clyde, Joe notices that the corporation has hired a new public relations outfit in order to promote itself as "citizens concerned about the environment." This makes Joe even more anxious.

THE NATURE OF WHISTLE-BLOWING

The simplest, and most literal, kind of whistle-blowing is always regarded as morally appropriate. If a thief steals a handbag from an elderly woman, and a whistle is blown to alert a nearby police officer, all agree that the act of warning was virtuous. In fact, such whistle-blowing is cause for honors and rewards, perhaps even a parade!

We also view the failure to attend to the manifest needs of vulnerable others as morally insufficient. The woman being sexually assaulted, while a dozen others look on, is justified in asking (later on): "Where were the whistle-blowers? Why didn't somebody help me?" In general—and the law of negligence affirms this—the duty to aid another depends upon our relationship to that other person. Parents cannot abandon their children. You must not leave an injured passenger in your car and go out for a drink. We are obliged, legally and morally, to make good on our promises and contracts.

But what kind of obligation do we have to strangers? Or to that mass of unknown persons, the public? Moreover, do professional accountants have special duties in this area by virtue of their professional status? Can there be loyalty to impersonal corporations, or to governmental bodies? When we see the woman being assaulted, the options seem real, clear, and immediate. If we don't blow the whistle the thief will get away or the rapist will further harm his victim, escape, and perhaps harm others. But in the world of businesses and corporations, choices are less imminent and justifications harder to achieve. Loyalties are sometimes divided.

Joe Storms has a rich, and difficult, variety of choices available to him. Some are quite obvious. Joe can do nothing and say nothing. He can "sit on" the information about the environmental pollution and hope (perhaps) that the regulators will catch up with ZAP. *Or,* Joe could call a press conference and announce to the media that ZAP is a major polluter and that he has tried to bring about change from within and, having failed, he has no alternative but to "tell all."

Within these polar extremes (and we shall look at the ethical justifications shortly) are more subtle responses. Joe could go "over the head" of the plant manager and tell the district supervisor or (ultimately) the CEO about ZAP's practices in Industrial City and hope for immediate alterations. *Or,* Joe could tell Mr. Clyde that unless swift plans are made for limiting the effluent in the city plant, that he (Joe) will "go public." Joe could write an anonymous letter to the editor of the local newspaper. He could give a secret tip to the muckraking reporter of local Channel 6. Joe could discuss the matter with other employees, start a petition drive, meet with the local environmental action committee, call the city sanitary district on his own, or even sneak into the correct company office secretly to gather further incriminating evidence (for example, memoranda) and take them to the local prosecutor or to federal officials. Joe has lots of options.

We can continue to spin out plans for Joe—some have mentioned the possibility of having Joe appeal to the religious conscience of the plant manager by speaking with the appropriate member of the clergy—and can come up with some imaginative scenarios. But in essence, the moral choice before Joe is quite singular: will he blow the whistle or not? Will Joe take action to try to end the pollution or will he simply stop trying?

The choice boils down to a very personal decision. If Joe goes public, his spouse and children may suffer immensely. Whistle-blowers almost always lose their jobs; they are unlikely candidates for new jobs. To break with peers and with superiors is no easy task. Who wants to be in the media eye for more than one day? Joe is an average "accountant," not a "hero." But he is also a person with a sense of virtue and of social responsibility. To Joe, the continuing pollution is a lot like witnessing a violent sexual assault: it is *real*.

Considering our two fundamental choices—does Joe blow the whistle or does he not?—we find ethical justification on both sides. That is why this case presents an ethical dilemma worthy of consideration. But the strength of the justifications may differ, and an examination of the diverse perspectives may illuminate the case in unsuspected ways.

Let's make use of the hard-choices approach (see Chapter 1) in attempting to understand this case more profoundly. Step 1 tells us to look at the facts quite closely. This we have done in sufficient detail. Step 2 asks us to scrutinize the perspectives of the various parties in the case and to distinguish ethical from legal viewpoints. (Here we may wish to refer Joe to an attorney!) Clearly all of the officials of ZAP encountered so far have a single goal: to keep the status quo and to wait for the building of the new plant. Joe's perspective is quite mixed: a strong desire to do "what's right" combined with a vital concern for his, and his family's, well-being. Legally, Joe would not likely be prosecuted if he failed to tell his story in public. But ethically, of course, it may be a different story.

Step 3 asks us to state the principal value conflicts in the ZAP case. There are several. First, Joe is at odds with his employer's policies and practices. Second, Joe is at "war" within, conflicted about going public or protecting his family's security. Third, there is the question of corporate values—maximization of profit; having a good corporate "image"; pleasing shareholders and the financial market by selling the plant for the highest possible price—versus public values, such as promoting environmental health and disclosing dangerous pollution practices. Fourth, there is a conflict between present and future interests. If Joe does nothing, the practice will continue, but not indefinitely. Nevertheless, Joe should realize that the decision not to decide (one that often seems attractive in the midst of a dilemma) is in itself an ethical decision with ethical implications.

We are searching for an ethically justifiable course of action. Step 4 suggests that looking at our ethical systems may be helpful. Let us do so one at a time.

Utilitarian Approach

There exists no "cookbook" method by which we can balance happiness over misery, pleasure over pain, or good over evil. But in attempting to weigh the potential results or consequences, we commit ourselves to a utilitarian justification in solving the Joe/ZAP problem. Among the factors we should blend into our considerations are these: (1) Joe's personal situation, his family's economic status, their respective futures, the satisfaction that might emerge from successful whistle-blowing, the burdens that might result from an unsuccessful effort; (2) ZAP company's costs in having to repair their effluent management system, the impact of these costs on shareholders, workers, and consumers, the loss of corporate "image," the prices paid by upper management when the truth comes out, the extent of the damage actually being done to the environment, the fact that the new plant will do a better job, the increase in profits from the successful sale of the older plant; (3) public concerns such as environmental safety, conformance with regulations, enforcing corporate responsibility (and punishing violations) as a matter of both reparation and inhibition of future behavior by ZAP and *other* corporations or groups.

The utilitarian approach asks us to make projections of future behavior. This is always a risky business, but accountants are practiced at it. Let us try. Suppose that Joe does indeed go public by telling the press directly (not anonymously). The likely results might be these: Joe will get a lot of favorable publicity (at first); ZAP will get a lot of bad press; an investigation will proceed and ZAP's polluting activities will be substantiated; ZAP will promise to fix the situation; Joe will be transferred to a lower-level job or (more likely) will be fired; Joe's family will suffer, directly due to a lower standard of living and indirectly through the loss of community respect that frequently accompanies whistle-blowing in the later stages; ZAP will move out of Industrial City and prosper in the suburbs. Other elements of the scenario can be developed.

We may make similar projections about each of the alternative actions under consideration. Notice that we are creating a kind of ethical "balance sheet" with good consequences on one side and bad consequences on the other. Our desire is to find out by how much our ethical assets (good consequences) exceed our ethical liabilities (bad consequences) for each possible decision. We will find that in some cases the liabilities will exceed the assets.

How we make this choice will, naturally, depend upon the ethical weight we give to the various factors. Does the risk to Joe's family count a lot more than the embarrassment to ZAP that may result in better corporate behavior? Does saving some small water animals outweigh the need to discharge the copper waste "efficiently" and at a low cost? We can multiply such examples.

The ethical weighing and summing of probable consequences of actions is known as the calculus of utilitarian ethics. A satisfactory utilitarian justification of this case or any ethical dilemma will balance good consequences against bad consequences and come up with an appropriate decision that maximizes good consequences.

Deontological Approach

It is far easier to claim that "principles matter more than consequences" than it is to spell out just which principles ought to be affirmed in making an ethical justification. The deontological approach to ethical argument assumes that rights or duties are valuable per se, not because of the results achieved by certain acts. Some acts are wrong, regardless of the consequences; others are right no matter what the results. Value comes from principles affirmed and motives validated. But where do we find the principles to which we attach meaning and purpose? A clear source, of course, is religious and communal tradition. To speak the truth, to honor our elders, to keep our promises, to fight for justice—all these have biblical (and other religious) authority. And our secular society also affirms—in the U.S. Constitution, for example—our commitment to such principles as equality before the law and individual freedom.

In Chapter 1 we suggested one deontological system, that of W. D. Ross. We suggest that three of his principles can apply to the Joe/ZAP case: non-maleficence (the duty to do no harm); fidelity (the duty to keep promises); and justice (the duty to make sure that each gets his or her due—"just deserts"). Let us try to apply these three principles to our case and see where we emerge.

Non-maleficence is a prime motivator for Joe: he wants to make certain that harm is prevented; he is sure that ZAP is already acting in a dangerous fashion. A more positive way to put the matter would be to state that Joe ought to promote good even if it costs him his job: it is right, it is virtuous to limit evil and no one can state that environmental pollution is good. (The company has tacitly admitted this by enjoining Joe to keep his mouth shut!)

Fidelity comes into play in this case because it comes from the duty of veracity, the duty to tell the truth. Implied, or at least closely related to the duty to keep promises, is the duty not to lie or deceive others in the society. Veracity is rooted in respect for other persons or in adherence to religious principles. Ultimately it is the basis for all contracts and promises. Veracity makes consistency in social development possible.

For Joe, there seems to be some moral imperative to tell the truth in a particular way: to blow the whistle. He is pretty sure that this would be the right thing to do. But if he were to remain silent, would that mean that he was "lying?" Is saying nothing deceptive behavior? Are there not different ways of telling the truth? Or, to put it in more familiar terms, is honesty really the best policy? Were Joe to hold his press conference, without regard for the negative (or even positive) results, he would be pursuing veracity most strenuously.

Justice, which we intuitively think of as fairness, demands that persons be rewarded for their efforts and punished for their crimes. Justice is a non-utilitarian concept even though a just society ought to be one in which good predominates over evil. Fairness, equality of opportunity, equal access, and even affirmative action—these are concepts of justice about which philosophers and policy planners have long debated. Justice has a clear social dimension: Plato wrote long ago about the just society. But justice often involves conflicts of rights. My desire for a job may impede yours; the fact that I am not a member of a minority may disenfranchise me while it increases your opportunity. The question of justice creates ethical tensions that may find the same balancing problems found in utilitarian ethics.

For Joe, elemental fairness suggests that, were he to speak out about the pollution, he should in no way be harmed. Joe is an innocent (nearly): he has acted in conscience. But he has also rebelled against the company authority. He was told to keep quiet and he did not comply. Does *he* not deserve some sanction? Justice also suggests that ZAP not profit somehow by its arrogance or its disobedience to the municipal regulations. It affronts our sense of justice to believe that corporations can pollute, cover up, and somehow "get away with it."

The thing that makes this decision agonizing for Joe (and all potential whistle-blowers) arises from another Ross duty, gratitude. We would call it loyalty in this context—loyalty to the company and more importantly to the people who make up the company. Joe must after all relate with these people at least in the short run. It is this duty that causes the whistle-blower to pause and causes society to mistreat whistle-blowers even when their actions are just.

So we are left with the question of whether to report the pollution or not. The deontological perspective has not given a clear choice in the matter. Yet it has enabled us to think more clearly about the ethical reasons for alternative actions. Ultimately the ethical agent must make a decision based upon the weight of the ethical duties brought to bear in a given situation.

Ethical Realism

For Joe to utilize ethical realism in his dilemma, several factors must be present. First there must be a defined ethical community with well-recognized intellectual authority figures upon whose wisdom Joe might draw. Were Joe a member of the local chapter of the National Association of Accountants he might find support there. Second, these intellectual authority figures would have to have sufficient power and influence in the community as a whole so that their developed ethical values would command respect and perhaps authority. Finally, Joe would have had to buy into the values of these identified intellectual authority figures.

Joe might also be able to draw upon ethical realism if he were in a mentoring relationship at ZAP (see Chapter 5). Of utmost importance here is the requirement that Joe's mentor be a person who taught virtue rather than vice. In an organization like ZAP such a mentor might have limited influence. At any rate, if Joe does have a mentor who is a legitimate intellectual authority figure, ethical advice and counsel could and should be sought at that source from an ethical realism perspective.

It won't be enough for Joe to simply accept the advice of someone he trusts in this case. We demand that Joe be responsible for his own ethical actions. Ethical realism simply suggests that Joe examine community values for clues as to the action that he should take. These community values will either suggest Joe's correct ethical action or they will suggest that the community values need to be changed. Although nothing in the case suggests that Joe himself is an intellectual authority figure in the accounting and business community, nothing prevents him from notifying those who are. This act in itself might constitute the form that whistle-blowing might take.

CONCLUDING PERSPECTIVES

Whistle-blowing will always entail moral and psychological pain. Some will inevitably be upset; others will rise and fall. But in seeing the distinctions among the utilitarian, the deontological, and the ethical realism perspectives, we should not think of virtue as only on one side. Common sense is not a bad guide to action. If all of us acted upon our principles all of the time, productivity would grind to a halt as we hunted down even the most minor violators of our laws. Are there not better ways than whistle-blowing to ensure corporate responsibility? Could there be tax or other incentives given to ZAP to clean up its effluents? Though ethical calculations are notoriously hard to count up, we must also remember that when we make a utilitarian justification, we do so not only for the moment (act utility) but set a precedent for other similar circumstances (rule utility). What does it mean to say that as a rule it is always better for employees like Joe to be quiet? Or, on the other side, for companies like ZAP to be punished?

A principled approach to the ZAP Company dilemma *seems* to lead in the direction of whistle-blowing. If we can attempt to protect Joe from reprisals (guaranteeing fairness for the virtuous whistle-blower), the other axioms of moral behavior suggest that, in conscience, Joe ought to make public the information about the practices that are leading to environmental pollution. But what if Joe suffers? The utilitarian "worry" necessarily invades the proud declaration of principles. It is very human to be concerned about consequences. In determining a course of action, we naturally look to projected futures.

Does this mean that we can give no reasoned defense either of whistle-blowing *or* of remaining silent? We think that there is an answer to the relativist challenge. At the very least, we can state that, were Joe to keep quiet, he would be violating several important ethical principles; he would be acting either in self-interest or, because of an unmovable loyalty to his firm, benefit those who have already harmed others. From a utilitarian point of view, we can ask: "Would society, or even individual corporations, 'profit' in a system in which pollution were rampant and violators of the law protected?" Thinking things through, we often find parallel reasoning in the deontological and utilitarian formulations of a moral response to a decision-making dilemma.

The ways in which we conceptualize whistle-blowing tell us a lot about ourselves, our profession, and our society. Accountants, above all, are tellers of the truth. Their integrity depends upon independence and upon society's reliance on their veracity. Accountants who work for corporations sometimes feel torn by divided loyalties—to the company, to the profession, to their social responsibilities. If we support whistle-blowers, we may be stating that we as a profession believe that public values predominate over narrow corporate needs. If we defend principled whistle-blowers (like Joe) as a matter of policy, we proclaim our concern for the less powerful in an immense bureaucracy. We may even provide a check to bureaucratic power. These are ethical matters of far-reaching significance.

CASE STUDIES

4-1: GOVERNMENT CONTRACT

Jill Christian was pleased with her new promotion as chief cost accountant in the diesel engine plant of the Mega Tech Corporation. Not only was it satisfying to have the additional responsibility and authority, but the extra salary would certainly come in handy now that she was expecting her first child. And, she mused, wasn't it great that Mega had recently adopted that flexible benefit package that would not only cover most of the childbirth expenses but would also provide day care and flexible hours when she returned to her position. Yes, Mega was certainly a company that took care of its own.

On this day Jill did have one task that she was not particularly savoring. Ben Static, a foreman in the plant with thirty years' experience, had asked for an appointment to see her. Frankly, Ben was not the kind of person Jill liked to be around. A big, burly ex-Marine, Ben had the reputation of being condescending toward women. Jill couldn't imagine why he would want to speak with her and she felt apprehensive about it.

Ben: As the new cost accountant here, I want you to be the first to know that Mega is cheating the government.

Jill: What do you mean!

Ben: I've got the goods on them right here. These are photocopied time cards. As you can see they have been altered. All I know is that because of these alterations the engines we make for the Army somehow cost more than the ones we build for civilian customers. You're the fancy accountant; you figure it out. As far as I'm concerned, the monkey is off my back and on yours now.

After Ben left, Jill studied the time cards and compared them to the job order cost sheets for some of the government jobs. She concluded that essentially Ben was right. Overhead at the plant was allocated on the basis of direct labor hours. The army engines were made in a more modern part of the plant where robots did much of the work on the engines as compared with the more labor-intensive civilian engines. The alterations on the time cards had caused a significant amount of applied overhead to be shifted from the civilian jobs to the military ones.

John Love, the division controller and Jill's boss, was someone Jill admired and respected. John had been kind to her and supported her as a professional ever since she had come to Mega. She decided to present the evidence to him.

John: Jill, you don't know Ben like I do. He's testing you. This is simply no big deal. You know as well as I do that all the latest managerial accounting literature says that more realistic overhead allocation occurs when we allocate more overhead to more capital-intense areas of the plant. You're a competent professional with a bright future here. Don't let Ben get under your skin.

Jill: But the government contract. . . .

John: Those government bureaucrats don't understand accounting. Trust me, Jill; I've studied this issue. We're just trying to get a fair return on our investment for Mega here. We are family here at Mega. We take care of one another.

Jill felt reassured after talking to John. Yet when she returned to her office she couldn't help taking another look at the government contract. The language seemed pretty clear to her. The basis for assigning overhead cost on this cost-plus contract was to be direct labor hours.

Questions

1. Use the "hard-choices" outline to do an ethical workup for Jill. Clearly identify which of the ethical systems (utilitarian, deontological, or realism), you are using.
2. Would a different ethical system have led to a different course of action? Explain.

4-2: PARTNER GOES BAD

Jim Rice is the audit manager in a midwest office of a large public accounting firm. On his most recent job he has been pleased to work with Carol Merton, a rising star in the firm who is well known as the first woman ever promoted to office managing partner in a national firm. Moreover, he likes Carol personally and has been impressed with her grasp of the complexities of the retail industry in which their current client, Mystical Stores, operates.

However, Jim is quite disturbed to learn that Carol has decided to issue a clean opinion on Mystical. Jim had worked extensively on the receivables of Mystical and determined that they were materially misstated as to collectability. In fact, Jim even doubted the viability of the enterprise and had some doubts about the honesty of the smooth-talking CEO.

When he brings these concerns to Carol he is quite surprised to find that she turns hostile. She informs him in no uncertain terms that she is the one with the responsibility for this account and that he should keep quiet about what he has discovered in the course of the audit. She even broadly hints that any chance he has to make partner might be in jeopardy.

Jim is perplexed. Carol is not only the partner in charge of this audit but also partner in charge of the office. She is widely respected and liked in the national headquarters of the firm, which has received considerable good publicity for promoting her to managing partner of the office. The employees of the office are almost universally loyal to Carol. Still, Jim is convinced that issuing an unqualified opinion on Mystical is not just poor judgment but flat-out wrong. Jim does not know where to turn and is even considering "going public."

Questions

1. Do a hard-choices workup to assist Jim in deciding what action he ought to take. Mention each of the three ethical perspectives and whether you believe they would lead to different decisions.

2. Does the fact that Jim is acting in the capacity of a certified public accountant change his responsibilities with respect to this dilemma? Why or why not?

5

MENTORING: PROBLEMS AND POSSIBILITIES

The scene is the office of Bud Terry, a partner in a large national CPA firm. Bud and Davis Troy, a manager with the firm, have been working together on the audit of an important client, DOX Corporation.

"Well, Davis, that about wraps it up. I feel confident about issuing a clean opinion here. Nice job on resolving the potential inventory mess."

"Thanks, Bud, it was touch and go on the cutoff of that one large shipment. I'm glad it was resolved to the client's satisfaction."

"Davis, tell you what. This calls for a celebration. Why don't you and Judy join Joan and me for dinner at the club tonight?"

"I'd like that Bud. Let me call Judy to confirm and I'll get right back to you."

As Davis leaves the office he muses that this was the fifth major engagement in which he had worked under Bud in the last two years. During that time he had certainly learned a lot about public accounting from Bud. It wasn't so much the technical aspects. It was how to make your way through the politics of the firm, how to develop client relationships, how to balance personal and professional responsibilities—things like that.

Davis is quite happy about his relationship with Bud. He knows from the grapevine that Bud had gone to bat for him on more than one occasion with the other partners in the office. Not only that, he feels a deepening friendship bond with Bud. As he picks up the phone to call his wife, he realizes that even she is involved. Judy and Joan had become friends working together on a United Way committee.

Bud and Davis do have a close professional and personal relationship. This factor is rewarding to both men. To Bud it is a means of experiencing further job satisfaction after reaching the pinnacle of a successful career. To Davis the relationship is even more vital than he realizes in terms of his future advancement in the firm. To both men the additional payoff is their deepening friendship.

Meanwhile, in an office down the hall, Wendy Anthony is feeling frustrated. Wendy, a senior manager, believes that she has all the technical competence of her peers. Yet deep down she senses something is lacking in her career development. Wendy cannot say that the firm overtly discriminates against her as a black female. Quite the contrary, the firm has a progressive affirmative action policy. Still, Wendy knows that she doesn't have a sense of the pulse of the firm that her colleagues seem to have. She wishes she had a close friend at the partner level of the firm. Yet this seems impossible from a practical standpoint, since all the partners are white males and have little in common with Wendy other than the profession that they share.

DESCRIPTION OF MENTORING

In the above scenario the relationship between Bud and Davis is a phenomenon that occurs in communities, in organizations, and in other settings as well. It is called mentoring, a relationship in an organization that can occur between a senior member and a more junior member. The senior member is called the mentor and the junior the protégé. The mentor performs many services for the protégé, all of which enhance the protégé's status in the organization. This relationship has been described at varying levels of intensity by several researchers.

Most professionals and businesspeople view mentoring quite favorably. Nevertheless, this kind of relationship contains its own unique set of ethical problems. In this chapter we will fully describe the mentoring phenomenon as it is found in the accounting profession. We will then introduce some of the ethical dilemmas that accountants may face because of mentoring relationships.

Historical Perspective

The term "mentor" is derived from a character in Homer's *Odyssey*. In this classical work King Ulysses' trusted friend, Mentor, nurtures, protects, and educates Ulysses' son during the king's absence. The relationship between Mentor and Ulysses' son, Telemachus, goes beyond the teaching of specific skills. Mentor introduces Telemachus to other leaders and shows him how to maneuver within the social context required of nobility.

Mentoring has been around about as long as recorded history. The technique was used by the two best-known teachers in Western culture, Christ and Socrates. Both men gathered around them disciples whom they taught by their words and their actions. Yet the relationships were more than teacher-pupil ones. In both cases warm personal ties developed between mentor and protégé.

Mentoring was a conspicuous phenomenon in the prominent institutions of the Middle Ages. In religious orders, novitiates were taught the ways of the order by novice masters. Monks and nuns, once accepted into orders, placed themselves under the direction of spiritual guides. A man who wanted to become a knight did so by being a squire to an already established knight for the purpose of learning military techniques and the ways of chivalry. More closely allied to our modern accounting were the guilds. A man who wished to learn a trade did so by becoming an apprentice to one who was already accomplished in that trade.

Mentoring relationships continued into the modern era. They were most clearly evident in European and American military organizations where senior officers would groom young emerging leaders. Robert E. Lee, for example, was close to Winfield Scott during the Mexican War.

In the more modern history of the professions, mentoring has always played an important role. Until the early part of this century the best way to become a lawyer was not to attend the best school but rather to seek to read the law under a prominent lawyer in the community. The same practice was used in a younger profession, accounting. In fact, today we still have with us a vestige of this system in the accounting profession—the experience requirement for becoming a CPA.

Mentoring in Modern Society

In modern society mentoring has been described in diverse ways. M. W. Dirsmith and M. A. Covaleski have concisely described mentoring in a professional context as follows:

> A mentor does many things for the protégé, including: teaching specific skills; developing intellectual abilities; intervening and protecting to foster entry, adjustment and advancement in the organization; serving as a host and guide who welcomes the newcomer into the profession, shows him how it operates and introduces him to the most important actors; providing advice, encouragement and constructive criticism; and serving as a role model who exhibits appropriate values and a workable approach to professional endeavor.[1]

In the current business environment, mentoring is important for success. We can find empirical evidence of this from a survey of top business executives mentioned in the "Who's News" column of the *Wall Street Journal.* The results of this survey showed that nearly two-thirds of the respondents had had a mentor; one-third had had two or more mentors. Those who indicated that they had had mentors reported higher salaries and total compensation and were happier in their career progress than those who had not had mentors.[2] Other research has confirmed that mentors have considerable influence on the career success and satisfaction of their protégé. Accountants who work for corporations are subject to the same mentoring forces as their peers in other career paths.

Levels/Matrix of Mentoring

The term "mentor" has been used in business literature to describe various kinds of relationships at varying levels of intensity. C. M. Michael has greatly clarified the issue by developing a classification system for mentoring relationships.[3] This system is best understood as a matrix, which is illustrated in Figure 5.1.

We see that for a relationship to be a true mentoring relationship, two aspects must occur simultaneously. First, the mentor must be a person who has high power in the organization. By high power we mean that the mentor has substantial authority in the organization stemming either from her formal position or from some informal dynamic. Where the person providing the support has less than high power, the relationship is either sponsoring or career guiding, depending upon the amount of organizational power that the supporting individual has.

Figure 5.1
Types of Support Figures

Support Figure's Power in the Organization			
Low Power	Moderate Power	High Power	Emotional Closeness/ Intensity of Relationship
Career Guide	Sponsor	Mentor	High Intensity
Career Guide	Sponsor	Mentor	Moderate Intensity
Career Guide	Sponsor	Sponsor	Low Intensity

The other required factor for true mentoring is the degree of emotional closeness that exists between the two parties. As the matrix demonstrates, even if the supporting person is someone with high power, at least a moderate degree of emotional closeness must exist for true mentoring to occur. The combination of moderate emotional closeness and high power of the supporting person therefore provide limits upon mentoring. This is illustrated in the upper right portion of the matrix shown in Figure 5.1.

Rewards of Mentoring

The mentoring relationship is beneficial to both the mentor and to the protégé. The benefits to the protégé are perhaps more obvious. The primary one is career enhancement. First, the protégé learns invaluable things, both technical and organizational, from the mentor. These help the protégé in the quest for advancement in the organization. Second, the protégé is protected and promoted by the mentor. This is one reason the high power criteria is essential for a true mentoring relationship to exist.

A secondary benefit accrues from the relationship itself. The degree of emotional closeness criteria ensures that the protégé profits from the experience of forming a personal bond of friendship. Many mentoring relationships turn into lifetime friendships even after the mentor-protégé relationship is over.

The mentor also benefits from the relationship in several respects. First, organizations approve of mentoring relationships and thus tend to reward successful mentors. Second, many mentors have reached the stage of their careers where they have "arrived," as far as the organization is concerned. They will receive no more from the formal reward structure. At this point in their careers, guiding the career of a young professional provides the mentor enormous personal satisfaction. Finally, the mentor experiences the same rewards of friendship.

MENTORING IN PUBLIC ACCOUNTING

The existence of mentoring and the benefits derived from mentoring relationships tend to be more prominent in settings characterized by multiple management levels, committee-based promotion decisions, and an ever-narrowing pyramid of positions. These are the characteristics we encounter in large public accounting firms. Two research teams in particular—Dirsmith and Covaleski, and Cottell and Michael—have found large public accounting firms to be fertile ground for mentoring relationships.

These researchers have found that true mentor-protégé relationships occur predominantly at the partner-manager level of the hierarchy of public accounting firms. Fairly frequently these relationships develop from lower-level relationships such as sponsor-protégé relationships between managers and seniors. As the parties in the relationship were promoted, the relationship matured into a true mentoring relationship.

Professional accountants interviewed believe that the raison d'etre for mentoring is the "career management" of the protégé. One partner in charge stated that he believed the importance of mentoring for career management has increased in the last decade. Partners and managers agreed that a good mentor instructed the protégé on office and firm politics, gave advice, and directly assisted the protégé in managing her visibility and the perceptions of important others. In the partner-manager relationships studied there was an emphasis on behaving and being "partnerlike," with the partner serving as a role model for the manager protégé. Many partners believed that mentoring is essential to the long-run survival of the firm. We may readily conclude that mentoring plays an important role in public accounting firms in the socialization of professionals at the highest levels in the organization.

True mentor relationships are rarely formal in nature; they are not purposely planned, regulated, and rule bound. Some public accounting firms have developed a formal internal counseling program to assist in the development of their professionals. Several firms call these "mentoring programs." Many of the public accountants interviewed saw their firms' attempts to formalize the "mentoring" process as failures, primarily because of two factors. First, neither counselor nor counselee had proven to the other that he was trustworthy. Second, formal counselors were thought to carry too many advisees, nine or ten, contrasting with a typical mentor who has two or three. Both factors work against the formation of close personal ties. Those interviewed held that true mentor relationships arise only where the individuals feel "comfortable" with one another.

We believe that formalized "mentor" relationships, though perhaps valuable to the firm, are not true mentor relationships. Moreover, they rarely evolve into true mentor-protégé relationships for two reasons. First, most mentor-protégé relationships evolve informally with free choice on the part of both. Second, most true mentoring relationships develop a strong emotional component, and this is something that cannot be dictated by organizational hierarchy.

DEVELOPMENT OF MENTORING RELATIONSHIPS

We turn now to how these important mentoring relationships are formed in the professional community. We will point out in this chapter how the mentoring relationship has an impact on fostering professional values and virtues. Professional ethics are developed and nurtured through this process. While we stress the public accounting firm by way of example, similar processes occur in other business environments where accountants work. Figure 5.2 may be helpful in describing the development of a mentoring relationship.

The three circles in the diagram represent spheres of authority/influence that a high power individual (here a particular partner) in an organization has surrounding her. The outer circle represents what we shall call the sphere of influence. In a particular office any partner has a sphere of influence that extends throughout that office and over all professionals at the manager level or lower. Other more junior partners might also be within this sphere of influence of a particular partner. Persons within a partner's sphere of influence can observe her professional values. Those persons might adopt and cultivate those values and virtues, but they might choose not to do so. The partner cannot be ignored by those in her sphere of influence, but her authority is limited.

The middle circle represents what we shall call the sphere of imposed authority. Some persons within the partner's sphere of influence are within her sphere of imposed authority. They are there because the organizational structure of the firm placed them there, and therefore for them that particular partner is "boss." Persons

Figure 5.2
Spheres of Authority/Influence

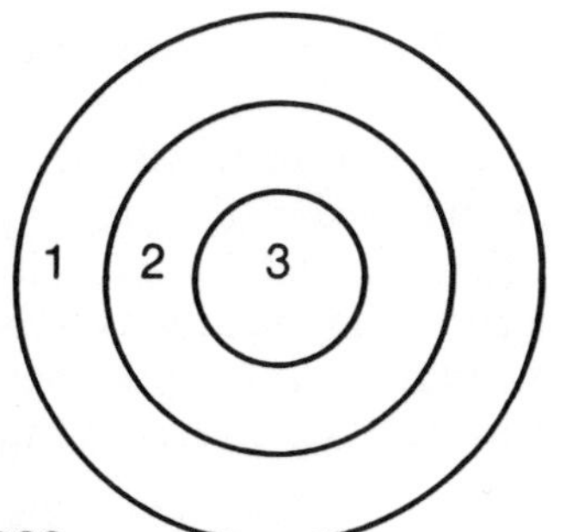

1. Sphere of Influence
2. Sphere of Imposed Authority
3. Sphere of Submitted Authority

within the partner's sphere of imposed authority must pay a great deal more attention to that partner's ethical values and virtues. Still, they need not adopt those ethical values and virtues as their own.

The inner circle represents what we shall call the sphere of submitted authority. Here a special relationship is taking place, the mentoring relationship. Persons within a particular partner's sphere of submitted authority have been "taken under the wing" by that partner. They are the protégés of the partner. The partner provides protection for those persons and teaches them the language game of the profession as that partner understands it as an intellectual authority figure in the accounting community. In a classical mentoring sense the partner is guiding the persons within her sphere of submitted authority toward success in the practice of accounting.

Unlike the relationships formed in the outer two circles, the one in the inner circle is completely voluntary for both parties. The mentor determines to whom she will give her efforts in the teaching of professional values and other kinds of support and protection. The protégé must be open to receiving the mentoring. For the protégé the mentoring partner is the one whom the protégé has chosen to trust as one from whom he desires to learn and receive counsel and support.

One aspect of professionalism learned in this context is ethics. Because of the relationship established, the protégé will adopt the mentor's ethical values in a professional context at least temporarily. For example, a particular partner may believe that the professional's duty toward the client is higher than duties to unknown third parties. Note that ethical accountants may hold differing views on this issue. Yet, if the mentoring relationship is a viable one, the protégé will come to hold the belief of the mentor. Rejection of teaching about ethics or any other aspect of the profession tends to signal an end to the mentoring relationship, since the relationship is by nature voluntary and the authority is submitted rather than imposed.

Not all accounting professionals enter into a mentoring relationship with a more seasoned member of the profession. However, the research of Dirsmith and Covaleski indicates that those who have succeeded in accounting usually have been in this sort of relationship. Most successful accounting professionals believe that the pervasive presence of mentoring in accounting is healthy for the profession.

Mentoring and Structure

Complexity can occur in the relationships depicted in Figure 5.2. A professional can simultaneously be within the sphere of submitted

Figure 5.3
Mentoring and Structure

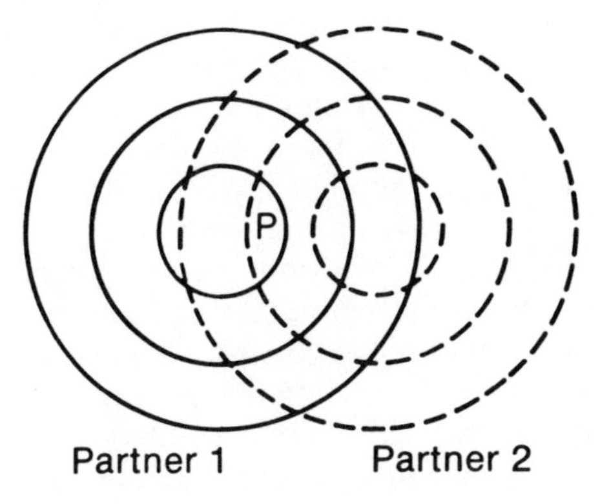

authority of one partner and the sphere of imposed authority of another partner. This relationship is shown in Figure 5.3.

In Figure 5.3 a mentoring relationship is represented between Partner 1 and a protégé who is shown as P in Partner 1's sphere of submitted authority. At the same time the protégé is shown in sphere of imposed authority of Partner 2. In other words, while the protégé is being mentored by Partner 1, she finds herself under the authority of Partner 2 in an organizational context. Note that Figure 5.3 attempts only to describe the relationship of the protégé to the two partners. The relationship between the two partners is not at issue here.

The position occupied by this protégé serves as an example of the sharp distinction that can exist between the formal structure of an organization and its actual day-to-day work activities. Such a position must be handled carefully by the protégé. Clearly she must take direction from Partner 2 in the context of the organizational hierarchy. Yet, if she desires the mentoring relationship with Partner 1 to continue, her loyalty and teachability must remain with Partner 1. The ultimate success of the protégé in the practice of public accounting may depend upon how successfully she sails these narrow waters.

The Exits from Mentoring

Because the mentoring relationship is a voluntary one, its termination can take on different forms. Indeed, different researchers on the subject have observed terminations that could be compared with the ending of a love affair or a time of marital crisis. These kinds of terminations are very stormy and can also be dysfunctional to the organization. On the other hand, an amicable and mutually agreeable parting is also possible. Many mentoring relationships end in an evolutionary manner and in some cases the friendship developed during mentoring becomes a lasting one.

Three reasons are possible for a mentoring relationship to terminate. The first is that the relationship has failed. Reasons for failure are myriad and can range from the protégé leaving the firm to the mentor withdrawing her protection and teaching.

A second reason for the termination of a mentoring relationship is a transfer of the relationship. In the scenario depicted in Figure 5.2, the protégé may develop a relationship with Partner 2 that evolves into a mentoring relationship. This could be a signal of upward mobility on the part of the protégé particularly if Partner 2 has more power, influence, or seniority in the firm than Partner 1.

A third reason for termination of the mentoring relationship is that the protégé is initiated as an intellectual authority figure of the profession in his own right. This is the most desirable outcome from the point of view of both the mentor and the protégé. In common language we might say that the protégé "has arrived." This arrival is in an informal context and will likely occur long after formal election to partnership or promotion to a more senior level in a corporation.

MENTORING AND VIRTUE

In Chapter 2 we discussed professionalism. Tangential to the concept of professionalism is the concept of good. By a good farmer we mean one who is productive over the long run because she practices excellence in agriculture. A good accountant practices excellence in the profession of accounting. In order to be a good accountant, one must have acquired virtues. "A virtue is an acquired human quality the possession and exercise of which tends to enable us to achieve those goods which are internal to practice [of the profession] and the lack of which effectively prevents us from achieving any such goods."[4]

Virtues are much broader in concept than attributes of success in a given situation. An individual's possession of a particular virtue would enable that individual to manifest it in different situations. In this way a virtue differs from a skill. The ability to aim a rifle and hit a target might help one to be a good hunter, but would have little use in accounting. Therefore this is not a virtue. Courage, on the other hand, might help one to be a good hunter, a good family member, and a good accountant, in that each could be more readily pursued by one who possessed this virtue.

The accounting profession as a community has recognized virtue both informally and formally. Intelligence and honesty are two virtues that are informally recognized by the profession. Independence is a virtue that has been formally placed in the code of ethics.

Ethical values and virtues are held by the intellectual authority figures in the accounting community. These professionals have succeeded in the profession and hold the highest positions in their respective offices. This does not imply that each one who succeeds in accounting possesses all the virtues. Rather, it means that as a group these persons possess all the virtues and, further, we would expect a successful individual to possess or at least appear to possess most of them. To state that a particular virtue is not found among the highest levels of the profession is to imply that virtue is not held by the profession itself.

The profession benefits from cultivating the recognized virtues and ethical values among its younger members, since accounting will not long survive as a recognized profession if the public perceives that the pursuit of monetary gain is its only aim. Values and virtues are passed along in the accounting community through mentoring. The close personal ties that accompany mentoring provide fertile soil for teaching the protégé to accept the mentor's viewpoints. The stronger the bonds developed in the mentoring relationship, the more likely the protégé is to adopt the mentor's values and virtues as her own.

MENTORING AND ETHICAL CONFLICTS

Mentoring, the very vehicle by which the language of value is passed along in the profession, can in itself be a source of ethical dilemma and conflict. We shall discuss several of these conflicts in this section: promotion practices, race and sex implications, the teaching of vice, and possible independence problems.

Promotion Practices

Most people in our society deeply believe in a system that Werhane calls "meritocracy," the practice of promoting a person because of worth.[5] We might even describe this as a twentieth-century myth. By myth we do not mean the popular notion of something untrue, fictional, or in the realm of fantasy. Rather, we mean a deeply held belief that cannot be proven or disproven by scientific method or other known systems of reasoning. The cornerstone of meritocracy is the notion that we ought to promote the "best qualified."

Our belief in meritocracy causes us to believe that somehow managers are able to objectively identify the persons who are most deserving of the higher rewards associated with promotion to higher levels in the organization. This objective identification comes from their performance on the job and their perceived ability to perform in the future better than their peers. As Werhane points out, this belief system is actually an outgrowth of Social Darwinism.

How does meritocracy find itself in conflict with mentoring in the accounting profession? Within the confines of meritocracy we find a deontological ethical duty—promote the best qualified. Yet the choice of who to mentor made by high-levels partners in CPA firms and accounting managers in corporations does not result from a systematic search for the best qualified protégé. Rather the mentor-protégé relationship evolves during personal interaction and contact on the job.

One of the functions of the mentor is to look after the interests of the protégé in the world of office politics. Personal loyalty and friendship are paramount values here. In this we have another ethical duty that is at least closely allied with Ross's fidelity. An implied if not implicit promise of protection and advancement is present in the mentoring relationship. In this environment the duty of fidelity will inevitably find itself in conflict with the value of promoting the best qualified.

Race and Sex Implications

Mentoring can also cause conflict with another widely held value in our society, freedom from bias based upon race, sex, religion, and so forth. In the perfect society we are all color-blind, sex-blind, and all the rest. Yet something in our nature seems to cause people of similar rather than diverse cultural, racial, and other backgrounds to associate. Because of this we are not surprised to find mentors and protégés to be from similar backgrounds. This is not blatant racism or sexism. Rather it is insidious and occurs because of the evolutionary nature of the mentoring relationship. Mentoring also interacts with sexual static, which we address more fully in Chapter 9.

When we add to this that until twenty-five years ago our profession was the nearly exclusive domain of white males, we should not be surprised to find that mentoring is more available to white men than to other members of the profession. So the values of mentoring can be in conflict with the freedom from bias values of our society. Moreover, the benefits of mentoring may even be denied to blacks, women, and others at the time society has adopted the relatively new freedom from bias value. This occurs not just at the macro level but also with individual members of the society who hold to society's values, yet find themselves with bonds of loyalty and friendship toward a protégé.

Teaching of Vice

From the standpoint of the profession, the mentoring relationship can cause an ethical conflict when the values passed along in the relationship are not virtues but vices. While from a professionwide standpoint we believe that those who rise to the top in the profession are the good accountants—the ones who possess and nurture virtue—it is certainly true that at least occasionally an individual rises in the profession whose value system is not in line with the expressed or even implied values of the profession. When a person is in a position of influence and authority in the profession and that person does not possess virtue, it is still possible and perhaps probable that she will enter into mentoring relationships with one or more protégés. When this occurs she will pass along her values to her protégés, who will accept them if a true mentoring relationship exists. So from the standpoint of the profession, the good effects from mentoring—the teaching of virtue—can have a dark side we may call the teaching of vice.

Recently, a situation came to light where a prominent accountant, José L. Gomez, exhibited that his value system was not in line with what the profession would claim as virtue. Briefly, Gomez, motivated by personal greed, participated in a fraud in the E.S.M. Securities case. Gomez was certainly a prominent accountant with high power as the managing partner of a large office of an international accounting firm. As such it is quite possible and even probable that over the course of his career he had acted as a mentor of other professionals. These younger professionals could have adopted Gomez's value system—greed, lack of courage, lack of honesty, and lack of integrity—as their own. Most people would consider these values vice, not virtue. Certainly, these values are not the ones that the profession would want to promote. We discuss further implications of the Gomez case in Chapter 6.

The nurturing and teaching of vice is an undesirable side effect that cannot be eradicated in an imperfect world. The best that the profession can do is to minimize it by seeking to allow only those with virtue to rise to positions of influence and authority. As a community, accountants must do this because the alternative is the loss of status in society as a profession, should the public perceive that the values of the profession are not in fact virtue but vice.

Independence Implications

The close personal ties created during the mentoring relationship have the potential to conflict with independence in certain circumstances. The accounting profession is one in which a great deal of professional mobility may be observed. Certified public accountants frequently leave their firms and take positions with that firm's clients.

With mentoring as widespread as it is, particularly between partners and managers in public accounting, the probabilities are high that persons who make these career changes are mentors, protégés, or both. The potential conflict with independence comes when people who used to have a mentor-protégé relationship find themselves in an auditor-client relationship. The conflict here will be more in the realm of independence in fact than independence in appearance. Since the relationships are personal and private, so too must be the resolution of any internal conflict that occurs. No set of rules will solve this dilemma. One must draw upon one's own ethical value system.

CONCLUSION

Mentoring—an ancient system found in a modern profession—is for the most part a powerful force for good. Most people in the profession view mentoring in a highly favorable light, and rightly so. Mentoring is an efficient way for the accounting culture to pass along all the experience, wisdom, and value so necessary for the profession to exist as we know it. While the potential for ethical conflict does exist, as long as the profession itself values its own ethical stance, mentoring has greater potential to foster ethics than to harm it.

CASE STUDIES

5-1: ETHICS AND MENTORING

John is a partner in a large national CPA firm. His current position is managing partner of the Toledo office. John is preparing for a partners' meeting in New York. One of the items on the agenda is to decide which of two senior mangers currently under consideration will be admitted to partnership at the Detroit office.

John has reviewed the files of both managers, James and Paul. He grudgingly admits that the two men have nearly identical credentials.

John is a strong supporter of affirmative action in his firm and, since Paul is black, John would normally support him for promotion under these circumstances. However, the circumstances in this case are not normal. Because of the special relationship that John and James share, John is preparing to go into the New York meeting and fight with all the resources at his disposal for the promotion of James.

John had met James a number of years ago when they were both in the Detroit office. At the time, John was a newly promoted partner and James was a seasoned senior accountant. They were on a small engagement together out of town when John noticed what he considered star quality in James. John decided that he would make a special effort to befriend James and help him in his professional career. James proved to be a willing and grateful student of the instruction and help that John offered.

During the years that followed, John taught James everything that he knew about auditing, client relations, internal firm politics, and the profession in general. John made a point of ensuring that James was introduced to the key players in the firm and in the city, watched out for his interests in personnel matters in the firm, and was instrumental in his early promotion to manager.

John's relationship with James extended far beyond the workplace. John had shared his faith with James and because of this James had converted to Christianity. James decided to attend the same church as John and they even went to a small group Bible study together. The wives of the two men got along as well, and John and his wife started to invite James and his family to vacation with them at their cabin in northern Michigan.

The friendship of the two men had continued almost undisturbed even after John's promotion and move to the Toledo office. This past spring John and James had gone to the cabin by themselves before the tourist season started and had cut firewood on the property and done other chores together in anticipation of opening the cabin during the summer. During that time James had confided in John that he was quite anxious about his impending promotion and the two had discussed strategy together.

John mused that the younger man had become the best friend that he had. John had also received a great deal from the relationship since James's phenomenal success in public accounting gave John a great deal of internal satisfaction.

John knew that it could be an uphill battle on promotion this time, yet he was prepared to pull out all the stops on this one. Besides, he reasoned, Paul was sure to make partner during the next go-around anyway.

Questions

1. What ethical dilemmas do you see in mentoring relationships? Suggest ways to resolve them using ethical constructs.
2. Under what conditions, if any, do you believe affirmative action considerations should come into play in a professional context?

5-2: MENTOR-PROTÉGÉ CONFLICT

Steve Showgren is a junior-level partner with a large international accounting firm. Steve's office is in a large metropolitan area and the firm has high visibility in the community.

During the last few years Steve has been involved in a mentoring relationship with Pete Gamble, who is presently managing partner of the office where Steve works. Steve is an accountant with considerable ability and motivation. Nevertheless, his promotion to partner early in his career is at least partially due to Pete's considerable influence with the firm at the national level.

Over the years, the relationship between Steve and Pete has become quite close personally as well as professionally. Steve has learned a great deal about the profession from Pete and has adopted many of Pete's professional values as his own.

Another aspect of Steve's life is his strong religious conviction. In this context, Steve believes strongly that he has a moral duty to feed the poor of the city. He therefore is active in a church that has a major ministry in the inner city distributing food to needy persons. Steve spends much of his free time engaged in this ministry.

During this year's annual review, the following conversation ensued between Pete and Steve:

Pete: Well, Steve, this has been another banner year for you. You not only greatly expanded your client base, but also brought in several MAS jobs from audit clients. Congratulations.

Steve: Thanks, Pete.

Pete: You know, Steve, I firmly believe that you are on track to reach the highest levels of the firm. Because of that I want you to get more involved with charitable work in the community to increase your visibility.

Steve: But Pete, you know I already spend most of my free time on charitable activities.

Pete: Ah, yes, that feeding the poor stuff. Steve, that's all well and good, but how many clients do you think you are going to meet in the inner city? I think you should switch your emphasis. I believe that I can get you a ground-level volunteer job at the art museum. If you spend as much time there as you do fooling around with that church, you'll soon be on the board. Now that's visibility! A lot of potential clients are actively involved with that museum. Plus you've got to admit that the museum is certainly a worthy cause.

Questions

1. If Steve decides to continue with his activities among the poor, what effect do you foresee with respect to his career? What signal might be sent with respect to the mentor-protégé relationship?
2. What ethical conflicts do you see in this case? Would utilitarian, deontological, and realism ethical models suggest different ethical resolution of the conflicts?

NOTES

1. M. W. Dirsmith and M. A. Covaleski, "Informal Communications, Nonformal Communications, and Mentoring in Public Accounting Firms," *Accounting, Organization and Society*, May 1985, p. 157.

2. G. R. Roche, "Much Ado about Mentors," *Harvard Business Review*, January/February 1979.

3. C. M. Michael, "Support Relationships in the Career Development of Home Economists in the Home Equipment and Related Product Industries," *Home Economics Research Journal*, March 1988.

4. A. C. McIntyre, *After Virtue*, 2nd ed. (Notre Dame, Ind.: University of Notre Dame Press, 1984), p. 191.

5. P. H. Werhane, "Sexual Static and Idea of Professional Objectivity," in A. R. Gini and T. Sullivan, eds., *It Comes with the Territory: An Inquiry Concerning Work and the Person* (New York: Random House, 1989).

6

LAW AND ETHICS: ILLEGAL ACTIONS AND HARM TO SOCIETY

INTRODUCTION: THE GOMEZ CASE

On March, 4, 1987, José L. Gomez surrendered himself to begin a twelve-year prison term. Gomez, thirty-nine years old, pleaded guilty to several charges pertaining to his role in the fraud of E.S.M. Securities, the Fort Lauderdale, Florida, firm that had perpetrated one of the biggest financial scandals of the past decade. Gomez, a managing partner of the Grant Thornton accounting firm at the time of his arrest, admitted to having knowingly attested to E.S.M.'s false financial statements for five years. He was the partner in charge of the company's audit during this period.

Gomez seemed, at the surface, to be the "wrong" kind of character in this accounting morality play. He was no demon. On the contrary, Gomez was a model of corporate success, was active in community affairs, had a long and healthy marriage, and was proud of his two young sons. That he could be a principal player in a fraud scheme in which investors eventually lost some $320 million was a surprise to many, including José L. Gomez.

As he was about to go to prison, Gomez told the *Wall Street Journal* that when he began to cross the line from ethical responsibility to illegal activity he felt he "had a terrific career path in front of me and a lot of ambition."[1] The story of Gomez and E.S.M.—and the strange mix of personal desire and social consequence in it—illustrates most of the problems accountants face in obeying the law and acting ethically in the face of pressures from a variety of sources.

CONFLICTING LOYALTIES

The law is a guarantor of social stability. If driving were not regulated we could choose which side of the street to drive on or mount the sidewalk when convenient. The law provides for collective safety and security. But it has more than a stabilizing function for society—it also embodies values. Telling the truth is the root of all contracts. It is also fundamental to criminal law; that is why we swear (sometimes on the Bible) to be honest in a criminal trial. The law reflects our social mores: school desegregation is an illustration. And often the law demonstrates our imperfections and uncertainties. That is why affirmative action is such a controversial topic. Our society, and thus our law, is not yet settled on this difficult problem.

The law, above all, embodies social principles, ideals that must not be violated easily or at all. Just as biblical authority tell us, "thou shalt not steal," so does secular law prohibit burglary and theft. We could not live in a community in which taking what one wants had no consequences. So the law is both a set of structures for social stability and a set of moral guideposts. When the law is broken, we see, in the cases that reach a court, the moral drama of a society trying to right a wrong.

Individuals rarely cross the border from legal to illegal behavior. But crime *is* a fact of our everyday life. Murder, rape, kidnapping, robbery, assault—these are widely publicized and often the growth of such crime creates anxiety (FBI statistics are widely printed; some cities are clearly "safer" than others). But crime that is at once less violent, and less publicized, has (until quite recently) not been a source of much social concern. During the past decade, however, this so-called white-collar crime has moved toward the center of the social agenda. The E.S.M. scandal was a clear manifestation of that concern.

Street criminals usually have a very singular motive: they grab a purse or wallet in order to get money, perhaps to buy drugs or to enrich themselves. Persons who act violently—who murder, for example—have many, or mixed, motives. Family conflict may erupt into a stabbing. Psychological stress may precipitate an emotional outburst leading to assault. On rare occasions, violence may be the result of a major mental illness.

But in the realm of white-collar crime—in which personal enrichment is surely a major factor—there are also motivational complications. A major dimension of white-collar crime, one especially pertinent to working accountants who daily face the temptations of altering information in the pursuit of gain, is the factor of divided loyalties.

Accountants are, of course, obligated to obey the law and to "refrain from engaging in any activity that would prejudice their ability to carry out their duties ethically."[2] This generic requirement, or another version mandated by AICPA Rule 102 on "Integrity and Objectivity,"[3] is a significant authority. But the opportunities and temptations do not vanish through the promulgation of codes.

Loyalty to the truth—embodied in the very notion of objectivity—is fundamental to accounting. But there are other, often competing, loyalties, especially for the young practitioner "on the way up." Since the 1960s, for example, accounting firms have placed emphasis upon marketing as a function of the firm. While auditing may be the "bread and butter" of an accounting organization, increasingly we find that consulting is where the profits lie in the accounting profession. In fact, concern has frequently been expressed that competitive pressure, particularly price competition, is reducing the audit to a mere commodity. With pride in a quality audit and the attending external and internal rewards in danger of extinction, the audit could be reduced to nothing more than a means to entry for lucrative management advisory service work.

There are many other "masters" to serve. To be successful one must be productive; one must "get along with" one's superiors in the accounting firm; one must demonstrate expertise, sophistication, and drive. In dealings with the client, one must tread the fine line between telling the truth and *not* completely alienating a source of income and networking opportunities. Above all, the internal "master" of ambition exercises its power. Thought and reflection on matters of law and ethics sometimes come in at last place when ambition is excessive.

José Gomez says that his ambition drove him awry, that he crossed the line into criminality without even realizing it. Gomez says that, just a few days after he was made a partner in his accounting firm, two officers of E.S.M. told him about a crude accounting ruse that was hiding millions of dollars in losses. Gomez claims that in earlier audits he had missed this ruse and had signed off, erroneously, on what amounted to two bogus financial statements. He states that one of the E.S.M. officers used that error to draw him into the fraud.

Believing that his innocent acknowledgment of having aided in a fraud would limit, if not ruin, his career, Gomez equivocated. E.S.M. asked for some "time," and instead of going immediately to his accounting colleagues—or threatening to blow the whistle—Gomez decided to wait. He had just been promoted to partner. He decided to "think about it. And a day or two later, I felt I already had gone too far." He turned his face away from his responsibilities, he said.

Bartels speaks about the many directions in which, in our pluralistic society, a professional is pulled. Trying to balance "obligations and satisfactions" happens only ideally. But most of the time, doing right in a situation of contradiction and dilemma is "impossible."[4] The loyalties of Gomez were disparate and, almost without malice, he was caught in a trap partially of his own making.

THE ETHICAL "SELF"

It is naive to believe that any single person is completely ethical all of the time. Such persons, if they do exist, have exceeded all we know about human personality. As George Orwell once said about such secular saints, they should be deemed guilty until proven innocent. Still, as professionals and as citizens, we claim a desire to behave as ethically as possible. And when it comes to the impacts of our actions, we seek to do as little harm as possible and to promote social good whenever feasible.

How do we try to create an ethical "self," a personality and set of behaviors that naturally obeys the law and observes the usual principles of the social compact? Or, conversely, how do we try to head off the temptation to become ethically repugnant? These are complex psychological and developmental questions. We need not go into the details of the psychology of moral development to note that such development comes gradually, through childhood and adolescence, and that much evidence suggests the ways in which we conceptualize right and wrong conduct seem linked to male and female characteristics.[5] Who we are and how we were reared are very important factors.

Despite these factors, for most adults, more is required in order to become an ethical "self." Three dimensions of consciousness and conduct seem indispensable.

A Belief in Values

If we hold that all actions are equally valuable, or if we claim that all systems of moral evaluation are equal in status and power, we are in deep trouble. A complete ethical relativism is almost unworkable. If one says that "experimenting on humans, using torture as a means of behavior modification, is all right if you can get away with it," then we run into deep moral difficulty. There can be no sustained human conversation when all is permitted on the grounds of "that's your view and it's fine by me." At a bare minimum we judge moral conduct on its impact: if it harms many in an avoidable manner, we are likely to censure it.

But beyond this minimum, a belief in ethics entails a non-empirical concern for values. There is no scientifically verifiable way to validate moral claims. Ethical statements are not proven in the same way as, say, a surveyor's predictions about land borders. In order to be ethical, we must have some kind of faith—and it definitely need not be religious in the conventional sense—that values count.

A Capacity to Reflect

If we go through life as if it were an automatic process, we will never take the time or energy—and both are required—to ask ourselves hard questions. Why is this action right, or wrong? What is the meaning of the work I am doing? Who is really affected by my decisions? What is my relationship to my colleagues, family, friends, and the wider society? These very fundamental questions demand ethical reflection. They ask us to stop and ponder, to use the tools of reason, to think and to participate in an "internal dialogue." As the philosopher Hannah Arendt once said, doing philosophy (or ethics) is nothing more than "thinking what we are doing." Reflection is both a psychological and a moral activity. It asks us to gain a bit of distance from our everyday needs and to see ourselves as others might if they had access to our innermost thoughts. Reflection entails self-criticism, a very hard thing to do. We are often caught by a desire to see ourselves as inherently virtuous, reinforced by that other very human attribute, the capacity for self-deception. But a commitment to reflection is clearly basic to creating an ethical "self."

A Sense of Community

Though the United States is a highly individualistic society, it is ethically dangerous to always, and exclusively, think of oneself. We are, by definition, social animals. We are born into families and often recreate them; we work, and play, with others; we participate in the democratic process, which presupposes a commitment to collaboration. And we usually define our problems and their solutions in a social way. When we want our highways repaved, we do not hire our own steamroller; we find a way to create the common good together. Ethical egoism—the notion that what is right is what I believe right for me—is clearly a very narrow and selfish point of view. Some libertarians take only a slightly more social position, claiming that all individuals are free to pursue their self-interest, unless others are harmed. Yet even here a sense of social obligation is already entailed.

We feel that a minimum of concern for others is required for the moral personality. A sense of reciprocity and of potential collaboration suggests what sociologists have long known—that we are social beings and we can thrive only *with* others. The hermit or the Superman is more a creature of fantasy. A sense of loyalty to others, and to the body politic, means that we must respect the principles of collaboration, especially the deontological dictum never to treat others as means to our own ends. It also means that we must calculate the consequences of our actions with a mind toward maximizing the good for the many, and not just for ourselves. This sense of moral community, of course, is the basis of most organized religions, though one need have no special proclivity toward orthodoxy in order to develop a sense of social responsibility.[6]

PROTECTING OTHERS

For accountants, conflicts emerge when countervailing claims force a dilemma. If an employer begs, "don't tell this time; I had no choice but to act unethically," the subordinate is thrust into a grave difficulty. If he respects the request, ethically unsound behavior is seconded. If he disregards the statement, a job might be lost, a family might be placed in financial jeopardy. But these are only the local manifestations of the dilemma. What about those unknown faces—consumers, other companies, political bodies, the public at large—who can be affected by one's activities? Accountants are obliged to care for the public welfare, especially the interests of shareholders and other "owners" of corporate property, by telling the truth and by resisting unethical propositions. When an accountant rejects a client's proposal of tax alteration or tax fraud, or when an accountant sees a conflict of interest or feels his independence jeopardized and acts responsibly—these are social acts rooted in a principle and a view of consequences. The principle is veracity (truth telling); the assumption about consequences is that airing a grievance will lead to conflict resolution and that all parties, including society per se, will be better off if legal and moral norms are adhered to.

José Gomez, and his downfall, are object lessons in both the notion of creating an ethical "self" and of the accountant's responsibility to protect others. Gomez was not a typical villain. He did not hatch a plot to harm others. He did not coerce people into a grander conspiracy. He simply kept the charade going and took advantage of the situation. Eventually, Gomez allowed E.S.M. to arrange loans totalling $200,000 for him, which were not repaid. Gomez says that he was overspending on his credit cards and that he was "looking to put a pool into my house." But he never viewed these loans as a payoff and claims that he "didn't do it for the money."

Accepting Gomez at his word—and we have no reason to deny his motives or his internal sense of himself—we can see some evident problems. His sense of values seemed quite underdeveloped. He sought to serve himself and his family, believing two things along the way. First, that he would not get caught; that things would work out. Second, that having gone so far, it was impossible to extract himself from a bad situation. He could not tell his superiors at his firm what was going on for fear of failure. Gomez seems to have had no faith in a very central accounting value: the confession of an honest mistake. A partner in his firm has commented, "I can't think of a partner who made an honest mistake who has been hung out to dry." Gomez had no faith in this proposition.

The capacity to reflect seems quite limited in this case. Pausing to consider the wrongness of his actions or even the likely results were he to be caught never seemed to occur to Gomez. His staff never caught on and he was not going to lead them in the correct direction. More significantly, Gomez failed to get outside his limiting desires and needs in order to ponder the meaning of what was happening. He knew, especially late in the game, that things were getting worse and worse. Yet he clung to the naive, unreflecting fantasy that somehow all would turn out for the best.

Gomez also had little sense of an obligation to the community, a concern for social good. The investors in E.S.M. would likely be wrecked by the scheme. Innocent parties allied with the perpetrators would most likely have their reputations destroyed. His firm would be tarred by the brush of fraud and scandal. But Gomez did not see beyond his individual perspective. No sense of social responsibility, altruism, or concern to public welfare emerged. And thus, Gomez did nothing to protect others.

SLIPPERY SLOPES AND PROFESSIONAL RESPONSIBILITY

The implications of the Gomez case clearly extend beyond the concerns of the E.S.M. investors or the personal tragedy of one accounting executive. We are quite naturally worried about other, similar situations. It is in the nature of successful frauds and conspiracies to remain undiscovered. Thus our attention must be directed not only to means of uncovering dishonest behavior. Ethically, we must learn to think beyond specific cases and to focus upon potential harm to society in every situation of ethical uncertainty, dilemma, or wrong.

Philosophers refer to the idea of unanticipated or unforeseen consequences of singular acts as the slippery slope concept. Simply put, ethical professionals must worry about precedents. When we were children we were discouraged from lying. Our parents delivered simple virtue statements: "Oh what a tangled web we weave, when first we practice to deceive." An alternative admonition stated, "Yes, you may not get caught shoplifting a candy bar right now; but this can lead down the road to thievery and jail." There is a lot of wisdom in these folk sayings. Most horrendous moral situations—like the Gomez case—started out "small."

Therefore, persons who think ethically look to the possible outcomes of even minor actions. They are also concerned with the meaning, for society, of seemingly minor choices that can grow beyond recognition. In the medical arena, the question of euthanasia entails such a slippery slope concern. Okay, we are told, it might be morally permissible to allow some very old and sick patients to die without surgical intervention. But what will be the next step? Will we encourage the elderly to commit suicide? Will we permit physicians to actively assist the dying of their geriatric patients? Where will the process end? These social anxieties follow whenever the morally problematic question of euthanasia arises.

Slippery slopes are, quite literally, unpredictable terrain. When that tiny snowball begins to tumble down the hill, we cannot tell how large, or how dangerous, it will become. Only when it pulverizes the innocent child at the bottom of the hill can we visualize the real consequences. The slippery slope doctrine says we should start worrying early.

Putting white-collar crime on the agenda of concern has not been an easy task. Only during the last twenty years has there been much press attention to the phenomenon. The political scandals of the Watergate era surely added fuel to the fire. Corporate crime—price fixing, illegal payments to foreign governments, tax evasion, and securities fraud—became a priority for prosecutors. Today there are also defense attorneys who specialize in white-collar criminal work. The media have taken up the banner and it is a rare month in which a story on embezzlement, fraud, or conspiracy in corporate settings is not featured on the television documentary shows or in the newspaper and news magazines.[7]

Exposés of dishonesty and fraud in accounting practice are, naturally, disconcerting to the profession. A climate of public trust and approval is shattered when lapses become known. But there is at least one benefit from this negative publicity. Professionals who might be tempted by opportunities for personal enrichment are given a tacit warning: *you might get caught*. While it is impossible to determine, scientifically, how many potential unethical acts are prevented by the reporting of scandals, it is a fair assumption that the deterrent effect of such publicity may force some accountants to look more carefully before tumbling down the slippery slope.

FRAUD AND GOVERNMENT INTERVENTION

"Where were the accountants?" asks the headline, in the aftermath of such scandals.[8] Assumptions among the lay public are quite clear:

- Accountants have access to damaging information well prior to any others
- Accountants pride themselves upon their objectivity, detachment, and independence
- Accountants have the capacity—many argue they have the moral duty—to send up a warning before a major fiscal crisis emerges

Hence the question in the headlines. In the aftermath of the savings and loan crisis of 1988–1989, such queries emerged not only in the ethics and accounting literature but also in the courts and in Congress. The Federal Home Loan Bank Board initiated ten lawsuits against accounting firms that had audited the books of failed savings banks. Three of the nation's top firms (Deloitte Haskins & Sells; Coopers & Lybrand; and Touche, Ross & Company) were among the defendants. The congressional General Accounting Office, having examined eleven failed savings units in the Dallas, Texas, district, found that in six cases auditors had failed "to meet professional standards." The chairman of the House Banking Committee stated to accounting industry leaders that the auditors of the savings units were "derelict in their responsibility to sound early alarms about impending disasters."[9]

It is impossible to know—prior to either public revelation, confession, or litigation—the extent of complicity in the role of accounting firms in the savings and loan crisis. The federal government pledged itself to "bail out" the affected institutions to the tune of untold billions of dollars. And the scandals will continue to unfold. What is certain, from the perspective of the ethics of anticipated consequences, is that one of the biggest financial disasters, Sunbelt Savings Association in Dallas, has cost the government $6.1 billion. The central cause of the collapse of Sunbelt appears to be the aggressive and unwise financial policies of its leadership and its bold and brash business methods—its fleet of seven airplanes, its expensive parties, its "cash for trash" real estate loans. During the three-year spending spree, the books of Sunbelt were reviewed by its auditor. The firm issued a clean opinion for 1984 and 1985. In 1989, the accounting firm issued a disclaimer for that year and, in retrospect, disclaimed the 1985 opinion.

The accounting firm responsible for Sunbelt's audit is presently being sued by the government. The suit alleges that the accounting firm failed to detect Sunbelt's numerous financial irregularities and poor internal controls. It also alleges outright fraud. The accounting firm, which denies its culpability, is Grant Thornton, the same firm that employed José Gomez, the central figure of the case described earlier in the chapter.

REGULATION AND PUBLIC TRUST

The savings and loan crisis, which many believe will have an impact on the federal budget for at least a decade, has implications well beyond the fate of particular banks, executives, or public officials. Individuals may be sued, successfully or not; institutions may be sold or swallowed up by former competitors. Legislators will, surely, hold hearings and attempt to prevent future occurrences. But the greatest impact of such a crisis is likely to be upon public perceptions of business practice and, perhaps especially, upon the ethics of the accounting profession.

The determination of just how extensive were the problems and fraudulent practices of the S&Ls will be made, in effect, by auditors. The Federal Home Loan Bank Board provides examiners, across the country, to investigate losses at S&Ls. How thorough will their investigations prove to be? Regional bank examiners have traditionally had a good deal of autonomy. But in a crisis of national proportion, image counts for a good deal. During the summer of 1989, banking regulators and members of Congress charged that the bank board was allowing at least one severely troubled S&L to shop around in search of the most lenient bank examiners. Parties involved in the audit differed in their interpretations of the events, but the public (once again) was forced to wonder about the role of accountants and examiners in the regulation of such vital institutions.[10]

Details about bank management are always hard to come by. The profession most skilled at laying out the concrete data is, of course, the accounting profession. If "politics" is suspected to have an impact on the truth-telling obligations of auditors or bank examiners, the entire profession suffers a loss of credibility. Thus, the difficulties encountered in dealing with illegal actions goes far beyond damage to individuals. It involves the moral fundament of accounting: public trust.

IN DEFENSE OF ACCOUNTING PRACTICE

The Gomez case, the emerging savings and loan litigation, and other cases too numerous to cite here, demonstrate the civil and criminal consequences of behavior that is either ethically wrong or dubious. But how far should the indictment of such conduct extend? This is the fundamental question engendered by the discovery of illegal acts in auditing and accounting. In defense of the profession, several points must be made clear.

First, the initiation of illegal and unethical practices did not originate with the accounting professionals. The greed and unscrupulous activities of clients preceded any accounting involvement.

Second, though independence and objectivity are basic to accounting practice, the sources of data—and thus the bases for financial intepretation—most often reside with the client. No audit emerges full-blown from the head of an auditor. In scandals such as Sunbelt, clever and creative duplicity of clients certainly contributed to the difficulties. If audits were designed to detect *all* fraud they would become prohibitively expensive.

Third, in swiftly changing business circumstances, it is often hard to render a faultless judgment about the financial health of a client. We render our indictments only in hindsight. Emergent conditions are always less clear.

Finally, we must certainly set high standards for accounting ethics. But they cannot be unattainable. We cannot expect more from accountants than we can, say, from lawyers or doctors. It is unfair to condemn an entire profession on the basis of several acts of individuals or even firms. Accountants are probably better at and more practiced at "blowing the whistle" than other professionals. We should not forget the myriad examples of accountants warning in time.

Still, the concerns that emerged in the Gomez case will never go away. Arthur Bowman, editor of *Bowman's Accounting Report*, says (regarding the S&L situation) that "some auditors may have been too close to their clients and allowed them to do things that they shouldn't have done. I'm not sure the industry was as independent as it should have been."[11]

Concerns for both legal and moral results must be built into the system of accounting. The slippery slope will always be there. The drive for success—for individuals and firms—will not dissolve. The only reasonable safeguard is to engender a sense of ethical practice in all professionals.

CASE STUDIES

6-1: REGULATION AND THE MANAGEMENT ACCOUNTANT

Pearl Terry has been employed by Farmers and Merchants Financial in Smith County, Kentucky, as controller for about nine months. She is delighted with her position. She came to Farmers and Merchants from a large national accounting firm. There she had been frustrated by long hours and audit assignments in which she had limited responsibility and challenge. True, she had taken a pay cut to come to Farmers and Merchants, but she now had a great deal of responsibility and authority. Moreover, her hours were flexible and she was therefore able to devote more attention to her husband and children while still pursuing a quite promising career.

Farmers and Merchants served a rural area of Kentucky. Its depositors were primarily small farmers and retired people. Loans were traditionally made to farmers in the area and to businesses serving them. The economy had been weak in this area in recent years and Pearl had been hired so that Farmers and Merchants would have a first-class control system to ride out these rocky times.

Three months ago, while reviewing the loan portfolio, Pearl had run into a disturbing fact. Loans to one powerful family in the area, the Bullocks, were hovering around 24 percent. This situation had occurred primarily because of some foreclosures on some of the small farmer loans that Farmers and Merchants had previously had. State law strictly prohibited more than 25 percent of the loan portfolio to be with one enterprise.

Pearl had brought her concern to the attention of the firm's president, Bud Olsen. He had scoffed, "'Pig' Bullock and I have been friends since we played football together thirty years ago. Those loans are as solid as the gold in Fort Knox."

Pearl was not so sure. Her husband, Robert, was the sales manager of one of the Bullock enterprises, Bagdad Mill. From dinner conversations with Robert she knew the slumping economy was affecting at least that portion of the Bullock empire. When she asked Robert about it directly he said, "Yes, times are bad, but I think we are going to pull through. I believe the chances of survival are about eighty-five percent. Those chances will improve dramatically if that bank of yours will approve a new loan application we will be sending your way."

Today the new loan application was discussed at a board meeting. Pearl had been surprised at the magnitude of the loan. She pointed out that the loan, if approved, would raise the percentage of the portfolio devoted to Bullock family operations to 27 percent of Farmers and Merchants' portfolio, clearly above state limits. Bud had stated testily, "Don't worry about those state bureaucrats. 'Pig's' cousin Sam works in the governor's office, you know. I'm sure you can come up with some accounting wizardry to keep the regulators off our backs. You're a CPA, aren't you?"

Pearl was indeed a CPA. She also was a CMA and had recently received a copy of the NAA code of ethics. The code stated she had to refrain from disclosing confidential information unless legally obligated to do so. Pearl believed that she clearly ought to report the facts correctly even though certain accounting "adjustments" could easily fool the state regulators.

When she discussed this with Robert he pointed out some things that caused her to further reflect. If Pearl properly reported this matter, it would probably cause a run on the deposits. Since the deposits were uninsured, this would ruin the lives of many small farmers and retired persons would suffer a great deal of harm in a time when the economy was already hurting them. Moreover, closer to home, both Robert and Pearl would probably lose their jobs and Pearl might even be blacklisted. Robert had told Pearl that he firmly believed all these evils clearly outweighed doing the right thing in an accounting sense. Besides, the expected pickup in the economy would bring in many new loans from small farmers just six months from now when spring planting started. Then the portfolio would be within regulatory limits.

Questions

1. Discuss a course of action for Pearl from a deontological, rule-utilitarian, and act-utilitarian perspective.
2. Does the NAA code of ethics provide sufficient guidance or support to Pearl in her dilemma?

6-2: RESPECTING THE LAW?

Arnold Seymour is a twenty-eight-year-old junior executive in the accounting firm of Kael and Shard. He has had three years of experience with the firm, having graduated from college after military service. Seymour is married and the father of twin girls, aged three. His present salary barely covers his family's expenses. Even with a working spouse, Seymour does not expect to be able to purchase a home for many years.

In the course of a routine audit of the Toscanini Record Company, a firm with seventeen retail stores in the tri-cities area, Seymour discovers that the vice president in charge of sales for Toscanini, Alvin Conway, has been writing some very interesting checks in relatively small amounts ($100 on each occasion). Seymour recognized the recipients of these checks—they are three local disc jockeys (for radio stations, WRIT, WEAK, and WVIR)—because he is a faithful listener to country/western music and he knows their names. A payment to a radio disc jockey for the purposes of promoting or "plugging" recordings is, of course, unlawful.

Seymour confronts Conway and asks him to explain the payments (Seymour has found eleven such checks, totalling $1,100). Conway is quite straightforward. "Everybody in the record business does it. In a small city like ours, if the DJ plays a tune three times, the kids go wild for it. This can mean a few thousand sales for us. And what's wrong with it anyway? No one is harmed. Kids will buy this stuff—or worse sounding things—anyway. This 'payola' stuff is from thirty years ago. It's a law which is outmoded. And no one pays any attention to it. If I don't persuade the DJ, then my competitors will."

Toscanini is a major client for Kael and Shard. And the argument given by Conway is quite persuasive to Seymour. In a city this size, the local prosecutor is likely to ignore such a "trivial" violation of a never-used law anyway. And Seymour's own future in the firm also crosses his mind.

Questions

1. If Seymour decides to ignore the checks written to the DJs, exactly what harms will occur, and to whom?
2. If Conway tells Seymour that the payments to the radio personalities were normal business expenditures—the standard sort of thing in the industry—what can Seymour say in response?
3. If both Seymour and Conway agree that the law is silly, outdated, and useless, is it not appropriate for them to "resist" this legal construct?

NOTES

1. The story of the Gomez case is told in detail in Martha Brannigan, "Auditor's Downfall Shows a Man Caught in a Trap of His Own Making," *Wall Street Journal*, March 4, 1987, p. 33. Subsequent quotations from the same source.
2. National Association of Accountants, *Standards of Ethical Conduct for Management Accountants, Statements on Management Accounting* Number 1C (NAA, 1983).
3. AICPA, *Code of Professional Conduct*, as amended January 12, 1988.
4. Robert Bartels, "A Model for Ethics in Marketing," *Journal of Marketing* 31 (1967), pp. 20–26, as cited in Don W. Finn, Lawrence B. Chonko, and Shelby D. Hunt, "Ethical Problems in Public Accounting," *Journal of Business Ethics* 7 (1988), p. 606.
5. Carol Gilligan, *In a Different Voice: Psychological Theory and Women's Development* (Cambridge, Mass.: Harvard University Press, 1982).
6. See Chapter 10.
7. See, generally, Stanton Wheeler, Kenneth Mann, and Austin Sarat, *Sitting in Judgement: The Sentencing of White-Collar Criminals* (New Haven: Yale University Press, 1988).

8. Leslie Wayne, "Where Were the Accountants," *New York Times*, March 12, 1989, Section 3, pp. 1, 12. See related story by the same author, "Showdown at 'Gunbelt Savings,'" ibid., pp. 1, 12, 13.
9. Quoted in Wayne, ibid., p. 12.
10. Ibid.
11. Ibid.

7

CONFLICTING MORAL DUTIES: SEEKING RESOLUTION

During the summer of 1989, the United States Supreme Court, by a divided vote of 5 to 4, ruled that a person who burns the American flag as a means of political or social protest is protected by the U.S. Constitution. The First Amendment, said the majority of justices, protects symbolic as well as real speech. The young man who burned an American flag on the ground outside a political convention in Texas should not have been prosecuted. The public outcry against the Court's decision was swift and loud. Claims of "they have gone too far" and "there has to be a limit to what people can do in making protests" were frequent. Members of Congress and the president of the United States began a process of constitutional amendment that would allow states to criminalize the "desecration" of the American flag.

Lawyers, civil libertarians, editorial writers, and many other citizens were alarmed by the vigorous negative reaction to the Court's decision. Defenders of the First Amendment stated that, though they might abhor the burning of the flag, they believed that the Constitution, and many earlier Supreme Court rulings, affirmed the right of the citizen to criticize the government (even irrationally). They worried about setting precedents—if flag burning is a crime, how about failing to stand up when the national anthem is played? These civil libertarians found an irony in the fact that to many persons the flag symbolizes the very Constitution that some believe allows for flag burning per se.

This illustration of virtual civil strife demonstrates the power of conflicting moral duties. It is often hard to know what is the right thing to do. If we can find a firm principle upon which to base our behavior, we can (at the very least) feel as if we are acting in conscience. But what happens when there is more than a single principle at stake? We affirm freedom most of the time. But suppose freedom is harmful to our equally fervent belief in national honor or an obligation to defend our country. The symbol of patriotism (the flag) demands our fidelity. But so, too, does our commitment to free expression and constitutional process. Is the solution to this dilemma found in passing the recommended amendment? Some would hope so. But others point out that the Bill of Rights—the first ten amendments—have never been tampered with. What sort of precedent might be set by such a "radical" solution to this conflict of moral duties?

When more routine conflicts of moral duties and ethical behavior arise—when the role of accounting professionals, for example, impinges upon one's personal values—the struggle for a solution to a dilemma is no less difficult. A homey example involves the case of Dexter, who used to box as a boy and now, as a father, has begun to teach his son the sport. Today, Dexter is serving not as coach but as referee. His own son is set for a match and Dexter does not want to give even the appearance of favoritism. But the match is a very close one. As a father, he seems to have the obligation to be a partisan supporter of his son. But as a "professional," that is, as referee, he ought not to compromise his objectivity and non-partisanship. (Many persons hearing about this case feel that Dexter should have declined to referee his son's fight.) What rule should Dexter follow? How should he resolve his dilemma? In the west of Ireland, a judge was on the bench when his son was brought to court and was found guilty of a capital offense. The judge resigned his position, but only after sentencing his son to death.[1]

The tension between professional and personal values is, for many accountants, a frequent experience. It is easy enough to ignore such problems, to regard them as "coming with the territory." It is also not uncommon to rationalize such dilemmas away under the rubric "when I'm at work, I am a professional and must behave in accordance with the canons of the profession." This is certainly not irrational thinking. But it does not eradicate moral doubts or feelings of conflicting obligations between professional and personal values.

One approach to resolving the conflicts of professional and personal obligations is encapsulated in the title of an article by Michael Davis: "Professionalism Means Putting Your Profession First." Davis argues that professionalism does *not* mean acting exclusively for the benefit of the client, nor does it mean acting in favor of some abstract ideal, such as justice or profit. Professionalism, he says, "ultimately rests upon a *contract* among members of the profession."[2] To be moral is to abide by the codes or covenants adopted by one's peers, or by their predecessors; it is to practice the standards of, say, accounting faithfully and consistently.

There is substantial appeal to such a claim. It would mean that, in a situation of moral confusion, one would only have to look to one's professional code or to the behavior of one's peers in order to find an appropriate model. But this advice is too general, too vague, and (above all) too unrealistic. If we could make certain and perfect rules of conduct for the professions, we would have done so already. All language suffers from imprecision. (Consider a classic example from the law—does the regulation that bars "all vehicles from the park" include or exclude baby carriages?) Above all, personal values and beliefs—religious convictions, for example—cannot be anticipated by codes or contracts for all professionals.

Conflicts of moral duty come in various shapes, sizes, and intensities. We cannot anticipate all such problems. But what such conflicts have in common is both situational and philosophical. By situational we mean that a personal moral dilemma is experienced by the professional accountant. She is faced with a concern and, often, a hard-choice situation. By philosophical we mean that thinking about essentials—goals, purposes, reasons—is ignited by the moral conflict. Confronting ethical dilemmas in professional accounting is a *real* task. The following sections of this chapter examine some, though clearly not all, commonly encountered conflicts of duty.

PROFITS AND JUSTICE

The economist Milton Friedman has stated the classic defense of the profit motive as the underlying commitment of the business professional. "In a free-enterprise, private-property system, a corporate executive is an employee of the owners of the business," says Friedman. As such she has a professional obligation to employers, shareholders, and colleagues to conduct business in an efficient manner. Put bluntly, Friedman states, the goal is "to make as much money as possible."[3]

But what of the person who is charged with the pursuit of profit? Friedman acknowledges that, as a person, he may have other obligations that he assumes voluntarily—"to his family, his conscience, his feelings of charity. . . . "[4] But Friedman says that individuals who pursue such interests do so not as professionals or as businesspersons but rather as private citizens. When they discharge social responsibilities or act in accordance with their own moral intuitions, he says, they are not acting as *agents* of the firm. And in pursuing their own interests, even if they are noble ones, they are acting unprofessionally. Friedman is an absolutist: a free market economy demands that business pursue a single goal—to increase profit.

But suppose that an accountant has strong feelings about helping the poor and homeless. He certainly can follow Friedman's wisdom and, on his time off, volunteer at a soup kitchen or (alternatively) join a group that raises funds to help persons on welfare. With community or church friends, he can establish new structures—a halfway house for recovering alcoholics, for example—that will alleviate suffering. All of this must be done privately, according to the Friedman mandate.

But let us also assume that our conscience-filled accountant is also a thinking, reflective person. Suppose he asks this question: does my professional role—and the companies I serve as an accountant—add to or help solve the problems of poverty and homelessness? If he were to conclude that, say, in his hometown the real estate firm he audits is involved in urbanization and gentrification and, as a result, its projects displace poor people from their low-rent apartments in order to build condominiums for the affluent, what should he do?

The scenario clearly depicts a conflict between professional responsibilities (auditing activities for the real estate firm) and personal morality (a desire to see that the homelessness problem is solved or, at the very least, does not increase). Principles and duties are at stake and seem irreconcilable. But there are strategies that, if not providing a convenient "way out" of the dilemma, do clarify (and sometimes make public) the conflict at hand.

The accountant can, if impelled by conscience or strict adherence to the deontological principle of non-maleficence (or, do no harm), resign from his position and make a public declaration of his resistance to any action that will create more homelessness. There is a long, and honorable, tradition of resistance to injustice. Think of the origins of the Protestant Reformation, when Martin Luther (in 1517) stood up to the Roman Catholic Church in the belief that the clerical hierarchy was violating divine law. Or consider, in our own time, Gandhi's willingness to go to prison for years in resistance to British imperial domination in India. Martin Luther King, Jr., in the American South, was willing to violate state laws that enforced segregation and discrimination. King appealed to conscience, to a higher moral law (or set of principles) that guided him and followers to non-violent resistance.

Does revulsion against homelessness create the same kind of duty to resist? Here, of course, individual moral sensibilities will differ. But one useful guidepost is what we may call a rule of proportionality. Simply stated, it asks us to reflect on (1) the nature and extent of the moral wrong we wish to see remedied; (2) the intensity of our desire to see change occur; (3) the benefits and burdens—to others, innocents especially—entailed in resisting authority or professional obligations; and (4) in a general way, the likelihood of accomplishing at least some of the goals we wish to establish.

Our auditor may, upon reflection on the rule of proportionality, quit his job and go to work for reform of the homeless situation. But he may also try to balance professional and personal obligations by taking a more moderate course. For example, urging officers of the real estate firm to read about the abuses of the homeless that are consequences of their gentrification program; arranging meetings among displaced poor people, city officials, and real estate developers for discussion of the problem; establishing a foundation to find alternative and affordable housing for those displaced; and so forth. This balanced approach—some would call it "middle of the road"—is not without difficulties. For this scenario is a complicated one. Surely the real estate firm's profits are at stake. But the accounting firm's profits are also at risk. For if the real estate firm, upon hearing this "balanced" advice, fires the accounting firm, no social change may ensue *and* the accounting firm will lose a client. The consequences for the individual, conscience-stricken auditor may also be personally disastrous: he could be fired.

Nonetheless, individuals and firms must, on occasion, ask themselves about the limits they think necessary in the pursuit of profit. Open, honest discussion of this matter will help clear the air.

SECULAR GOALS AND RELIGIOUS BELIEFS

If business professionals—accountants for certain—stopped to list the manifest goals their activities entailed, they might be surprised. If, in addition, they sought to contrast such goals with their own theological or religious beliefs, they might be disappointed. For example, an executive for a chain of electronics stores (purveyors of televisions and VCRs) might have as her goal the maximizing of sales of such commodities. There certainly is public demand for such goods; and, though most are imported from Asia (thus perhaps exporting potential American jobs abroad), this is not especially troubling to her. All in all, selling more TVs and VCRs seems like a fine idea.

But imagine this executive to be a religious Christian, one who takes the ideal of observing the sacraments and the notion of community very seriously. If she were to ask herself about the consequences of increased sales of such appliances, she might reason: "They are bought by families. But they reduce family members to passive watchers of more or less mindless television programming. And the video tapes available to our kids are sometimes quite objectionable, indeed pornographic. The overall impact of TVs and VCRs is even more depressing. We shrink into our little familial shells, never talk with our neighbors, and everyone knows that church attendance is sinking. Where has our sense of community gone? And don't our traditional values of friendship, charity, Christian service wither when we are all at home watching the tube?"

Here, a religious value system, upon interrogation, seems to conflict with a set of corporate or professional values. How can such conflicting moral obligations be reconciled? One can always suggest, "Okay, so take the VCR and TV out of your house, or limit hours, or monitor your kids more closely." But does this address the systemic question? How can this executive continue to work, in conscience, when her professional activities fly in the face of her Christian values?

One could multiply the examples. But, though nearly all of us tend to bracket our religious beliefs when "on the job," there do come moments of concern, even periods of crisis, when simply finding a local or immediate solution will not satisfy. Consider this illustration involving an accounting professional whose knowledge may prove to be a "dangerous thing."

Mary is an active church member. She has been integrally involved in setting up a day care center at her church. Part of the program of the center has been teaching the young children the doctrine of this particular church. Mary has several clients whose children attend the center. A new tax proposal passes, offering liberal tax credits for day care centers, but only if there is no religious instruction. This stipulation is based upon the constitutional principle of separation of church and state. The new law does not, in any way, prohibit day care centers from teaching religion; it simply denies clients a tax credit in such situations.

Should Mary inform her clients about this new law? It is her duty, as a professional accountant, to minimize tax burdens. If she does so, however, these clients may withdraw their children from the day care center. This will surely harm the center (there is no waiting list; indeed, the center is struggling to survive). Removing the children from this center—and transferring them to another, secular institution—will, from Mary's perspective, deprive them of religious teaching she believes to be indispensable to their moral development.

Mary seems trapped between her professional duty to tell her clients about relevant legislation and her clear, though personal, desire to see the day care center and its religious message thrive. She has several choices. She can, of course, act simply as a professional and take the consequences. (It is fair to say, however, that others—the church and the board of the center—will suffer consequences as well.) She could inform the management of the center of the new law and urge that they abandon religious instruction in order to be attractive to present and potential clients, from a tax perspective. This would, naturally, fly in the face of her religious and moral concerns. But it would, at least, guarantee the survival of the center, in the hope for better days (i.e., a time in which religious teaching is not "penalized"). Or Mary could simply remain silent and see what happens.

Any of these decisions entails difficult consequences. At the least, Mary should discuss this matter with other persons, including those who share her religious values, her professional standards, and her depth of belief. Is there opportunity, within the accounting profession, to share such dilemmas? Should there exist some sort of systemic support for persons whose religious ideals may come into conflict with the necessity to serve the ostensible best interests of clients?

LOOPHOLE SEEKING AND CHARACTER VIRTUES

Professional morality demands adherence to the law. But legislation, court opinions, administrative decisions, and (especially) bureaucratic interpretations of the law are rarely crystal clear. Because of this necessary imprecision, there are many opportunities to "bend the rules" or to "find the loophole." Such behavior, by accountants, is not inherently wrong. Nor is it subject to prosecution or condemnation if discovered. In tax accounting, especially, a premium is put upon creative interpretation of regulations (and of prior interpretations). The system exists to be *used,* we are told; a clever accountant takes advantage of ambiguity and resolves it in the perceived best interest of his client. This is normal professional practice.

In this realm, we are not talking about hiding data or obscuring documentation. We are describing a set of behaviors taught in colleges and universities and validated by professional activities. Yet if ethics has anything to offer the professions, it is an opportunity to consider, reflect, and criticize common practice from the point of view of morality. Here, many accountants would wish to proceed, upon reflection, with "business as usual." But what of the professional who, in conscience, cannot?

Such a person might say to herself: "If I continue to find the loopholes and structure my financial and planning advise based upon them, I will remain a fine accountant. But what does this kind of behavior, when practiced continually, say about my character? Can I be transformed in the process?" Looking at the same moral conflict from another viewpoint, we can ask the question, "If the law does not demand that I disclose information, will my morality suffer if

I, repeatedly, remain silent when information is relevant, though not legally required?"

Think of a company (let it be a large manufacturing firm, ABC Inc.) that is negotiating with a party (call it XYZ Inc.) for a potentially lucrative contract. An ABC staff accountant, in the midst of preparing reports and summaries, discovers that certain information about his own firm is not being communicated to XYZ. The ABC accountant thinks that the data is quite material to the negotiations and that the transaction will be affected by withholding such information. But the ABC accountant, on raising the issue, is told firmly and clearly, "Legal counsel have been consulted and are sure that there is no obligation, under present law, to disclose this information to XYZ." In this situation of legally approved concealment (let us assume that ABC counsel is literally correct), the accountant's professional obligation is clear: finish the report and leave out the contested information.

But the accountant's desire to give more than legally required information is not rooted in a personal compulsion to "tell all." It is derived, rather, from an elemental sense of fairness. The virtue—we can use this terminology, for it has a long history in moral discourse—of honesty and forthrightness is not sustained when we keep quiet in the face of "legal" requirements or permissions. When we are asked to compartmentalize ourselves, our essential being may suffer great harm. As many authors have said, a person who is courageous on the battlefield and a coward in business dealings is not a whole human being. The ABC accountant faces a very common difficulty: the expectations of management, in this case, conflict not only with personal concerns but also with internalized professional values. Here the accountant's almost instinctual obligation to make public relevant information has been headed off by a legalism that mandates concealment. Clearly, a discussion about the legal versus ethical issues would be in order.

SECRECY AND THE NEED TO DISCLOSE

To trust another person professionally and personally sometimes demands that secrets be kept. We introduced the notion of confidentiality in accounting practice earlier (see Chapter 2). But nuances and problems—conflicts of obligation—occur in this realm. The requirement that professionals of all kinds (physicians, attorneys, accountants, even clergy) preserve client confidentiality has two roots. First, promises must be kept and moral professionals must keep them. If one promises to keep a secret, this is almost a sacred obligation. As an early (1743) English court case put it, a "gentleman of character" (forgive the archaic language) should not disclose a client's secrets.[5] Second, confidentiality is necessary for the conduct of business. Professionals need to hear all relevant material regarding a client's activities. Clients will not disclose useful data if they feel that a professional will speak of such matters publicly. In business, especially, knowledge or information is power. And the privileged relationship between professional and client is a means to contain the spilling of information that may abuse power or transfer it to an outsider illicitly. Accountants, of course, have an obligation to report data and interpret it. But much that is secret is expressed to accounting professionals and they have both an explicit and a tacit obligation to keep such matters private.

The public reporting of illegal activities has been discussed earlier (see Chapters 4 and 6). It is certainly obligatory. But what about matters that are not legally compelled? The AICPA *Restatement of the Code of Professional Ethics,* in effect until 1988, is notably brief in its discussion of confidentiality. "It is fundamental that the CPA hold in strict confidence all information concerning a client's affairs which he acquires in the course of his engagement."[6] Of course, the AICPA standard does not demand that the CPA "acquiesce in a client's unwillingness to make disclosures in financial reports which are necessary to make a fair presentation."[7] This exception to the requirement of confidentiality speaks only to financial reporting. Interpretations of the rule discuss making exceptions to the confidentiality requirement when professional standards demand. This is remarkably vague.

Suppose, in the course of a discussion with a client, an accountant discovered a corporate practice that struck him as morally objectionable. Suppose further that the activity had nothing material to do with financial affairs, currently or in the near future. In a word, this confidentially expressed statement was never going to be included in or excluded from a financial statement. But, still, the data ran across the grain of the accountant's personal value system. Does professional responsibility enjoin the accountant to keep the secret no matter what? Is there ever a conflicting moral duty: to disclose, even at the risk of breaking confidentiality? Does the duty to keep quiet always prevail?

The political and social views of professionals do not, usually, impinge upon work-related tasks. But suppose the following scenario: An auditor is, for either religious or intellectual reasons, a pacifist. Her views forbid serving the military in any manner or cooperating in any vocation that encourages the development, manufacture, or distribution of military weapons. She is called in to participate in auditing a major corporation and discovers that the company is engaged in research likely to result in the development of a highly sophisticated new chemical weapon. Research on chemical-biological warfare (CBW) is clearly legal, though testing of such devices is strictly regulated and restricted.

The auditor has access to highly confidential information, though it is not classified by a government agency. Her beliefs are strong and clear: she should do *anything* non-violent to resist the spread of CBW. The mandatory confidentiality of her auditor role strikes hard against her pacifism. Though the auditor is not a company insider, she is personally connected to many corporate professionals. She is especially friendly with a vice president, a woman whom she regards as quite conservative (politically), yet open and supportive of change in the corporation. What should she do? If she discusses the matter with her pacifist friends, or with any other person, she has violated the rule of confidentiality. But if she stays silent, she has aided and abetted the cause of war, from her perspective.

Here again, the rule of proportionality may be of some service. Is the wrong to be prevented (by public disclosure) so very serious, and is the likelihood of prevention so great, that one can find a justification for violating confidentiality and telling about the CBW research program? It will be hard to achieve certainty in this situation of moral conflict, but the rule will at least allow the internal dialogue that leads to a decision to be sustained, reflective, and serious.

PROFESSIONAL COMPETENCE AND PERSONAL FEELINGS

The principal concern regarding competence for the accountant is one of individual conduct. Accountants should be well trained, and retrained when necessary. Undertaking a task when ill-prepared is not advisable. Working toward higher levels of knowledge and skill is clearly beneficial. Moreover, the code of professional conduct mandates professional competence in Rule 201.[8] It is obligatory for an accountant who cannot perform adequately to suggest to the client that another professional be engaged for the needed service.

But what about the competence of one's colleagues and, even, one's competitors? Does the general market principle of *caveat emptor* (let the buyer beware) govern? Does concern for professional competence —and the ethical obligation to disclose its absence—require the accountant to speak out about other professionals and *their* competence? In general, professionals, including accountants, are obliged by their codes to assist colleagues in maintaining professional standards and in enforcing code requirements. But intraprofessional behavior is complicated and draws from the professional a rich variety of forces and feelings, including jealousy, hostility, and vengeance as well as more positive feelings such as respect, concern, admiration, and loyalty.

The standard method of enforcing competence, at the lower and middle levels of most CPA firms, is practiced via the "up-or-out" procedures leading to partnership. If a person is not advanced to partner, he or she must leave the firm. This is the functional equivalent of life tenure in colleges or universities. Assuring quality and retaining the best professionals seem to make the partnership system a viable one. If a junior colleague (in an accounting firm) is, simply put, lacking in qualifications and seemingly incapable of improving her performance, there are, naturally, many remedies, including denial of partnership or, if immediate action is necessary, termination of contract. But matters are rarely so clear-cut. Consider the veteran professional—the partner long respected and most loyal to the firm—who is, for any number of reasons, no longer capable of maximal performance. Let us imagine this accountant to be nearing retirement age. "Wait him out," may be the conclusion, arguing that he will do little damage in the remaining year or so prior to retirement. But is this satisfactory?

The competence of colleagues may be compromised for many reasons: failure to keep up with developments in the field; substance abuse (drug or alcohol dependency); mental illness or personality disorder; physical problems such as Alzheimer's disease; or psychological difficulties such as marital problems, depression, or anxiety. The reasons may easily be multiplied. In each case, if a person whose competence is suspect is continuing to practice professionally, what is the colleague's moral stance?

Were a once-respected partner to become impaired as a result, for example, of alcohol dependency, what is the appropriate response by colleagues (either partners or not)? Referral to medical or psychological professionals is, of course, a desirable course. But one of the symptoms of alcoholism is denial. Working with an impaired colleague is demanding and difficult, straining once benign relationships, leading to impatience and anger. If the relationship with the impaired accountant has been one of friendship or mentorship (or one in which families have become close), the constraints are even greater. To whom is loyalty owed: the firm, the clients (present or future), the person presently impaired, oneself?

Is the profession prepared to meet the authentic personal dilemmas faced by professionals whose competence is compromised? The record of the medical and legal professions does not lead to great optimism. Stories of surgeons who have had to be forced out of the operating room are widely known. Will accounting professionals do better in confronting the moral dilemmas of removing a "friend" from authority?

A conflict surrounding competence can be quite profound if the allegedly incompetent colleague is also a personal friend or a mentor (see Chapter 5). But if the person whose abilities seem compromised is a competitor, additional difficulties develop. To bring to light suspected incompetence of a competitor invites an accusation of unfair business practices. And since competence is often subjectively assessed, it is difficult to maintain one's desired objectivity in facing these competing moral claims.

Complicating the interpersonal dimensions of dealing with competence, of course, is the competitive atmosphere, both within and among accounting firms. The AICPA has taken the initiative at the firm level in attempting to establish peer review, in which entire firms are reviewed by other firms to assess the quality of audit work. Such peer review has met with mixed success. Some of the national accounting firms have endorsed the idea; others, citing claims of client confidentiality, have resisted peer review. But it is clearly an item on the agenda.

There is perhaps only one certainty in dealing with the problematic area of collegial competence. Definitions and descriptions of competent work must be clear, consistent, and fairly applied. Justice—sometimes defined as the equitable and fair method of distributing scarce resources—demands that we treat like cases alike. But we should not use unalike cases for the purposes of unfairness or discrimination. The so-called "Mommy track," a personnel plan that recognizes the inordinate demands of family living made upon some women in a firm, should not be used as a method of accusing women of incompetence. Common sense and elemental fairness—and contractual agreements entered into knowingly and freely—should prevent the invidious distinctions that could work against women on the ground of "inferior competence." (See Chapter 9 for details.)

DOUBLE DUTIES

Ethical reasoning rarely results in certainty. One clear factor is the recognition that rights and duties, principles and beliefs, are often in conflict. Equality is a noble goal; but enforcing it can limit our freedom (another grand ideal). Devotion to one's firm is usually rewarded, materially and symbolically. But what happens when concern for one's country calls for behavior that may result in grave trouble for one's company?

Amendments to the Federal False Claims Act, adopted in 1986, provide for cash awards to company insiders and others who come forward with details about corporate fraud or contractual abuse. The law allows private citizens—and managerial accounts as well—to file civil suits in the name of the government charging fraud on the part of contractors and "to share in any financial recovery the government makes." The percentage of the financial recovery that can be given to the whistle-blower (most often an employee of the firm being sued) ranges from 15 to 30 percent.

Encouraging employees to report fraudulent corporate activities has a clear public purpose: to make sure that contracts (say, with the Department of Defense) are adhered to strictly and that quality is maintained. But in order for this program to work, employees must lead a double life. Divided loyalties and conflicting duties are clearly at stake in this situation.[9]

CONCLUSION

How do accounting professionals reconcile conflicting moral duties? In a fundamental sense, we can say that in practice they often do not. It is part and parcel of all professional activity to face ethical dilemmas and to experience rights and duties in conflict. We do not live in a homogeneous society. Indeed, in our century American life seems characterized by diversity and difference to an extent many find horrifying. As philosopher Alasdair MacIntyre has put it: "The most striking feature of contemporary moral utterance is that so much of it is used to express disagreements." MacIntyre laments the "interminable character" of our moral debates and believes that there is probably "no rational way of securing moral agreement in our culture."[10]

The recognition of the difficulties found in dealing with competing moral claims, however, need not lead us to despair. At least three positive things can be found in our recognition that accounting professionals do, routinely, encounter conflicting moral duties:

1. Consciousness about our common situation is raised when we make public, and discuss with colleagues and others, our moral problems.
2. Firms and professional organizations can develop policies and programs that respond to difficult moral dilemmas.
3. Recognizing that all professionals are also persons can alleviate unrealistic expectations regarding vocational activity and serve to humanize the profession.

In all of this work, it will be useful to make a careful examination of the styles of ethical reasoning that inform accounting practice, especially by giving attention to both principles and consequences.

CASE STUDIES

7-1: REPREHENSIBLE ACTIONS OF LOYAL EMPLOYEES

Nancy Beck is president of Kingdom Cup Coffee, a regional company that sells coffee to restaurants in Kentucky and Tennessee. Kingdom Cup is a family business. Nancy became president shortly after graduation from college when her father retired for health reasons. She has run the company effectively for nearly ten years. She has just learned through informal sources, which she believes, some disturbing news about her top salesman, Lyndon Johnson.

Lyndon has been with Kingdom Cup for over twenty-five years. He not only is the top salesman for the company but also has always proved to be extremely loyal to the Kingdom Cup company and to the Beck family. This news was therefore particularly disturbing to Nancy.

One of Kingdom Cup's customers is the Mountain View Country Club in eastern Kentucky. The manager of the club is Dick Nixon. Dick was the former sole proprietor of the Watergate Restaurant, which went out of business several months ago owing Kingdom Cup a considerable amount of money. In addition to being manager of Mountain View, Dick is the president of the Triple Restaurant Association, which wields considerable influence with restaurant owners throughout southeast Kentucky and northeast Tennessee, a major market of Kingdom Cup!

The news Nancy has learned is that Dick is paying off his debt to Kingdom Cup using the assets of Mountain View. With Lyndon's help, phony delivery vouchers are used to have Mountain View pay for coffee that it has not received. The payments are applied to the debt owed to Kingdom Cup by Watergate Restaurant.

Questions

1. What action should Nancy take? Upon what ethical basis can you defend your answer?
2. To whom does Nancy owe duty? From where does the duty arise?
3. If Lyndon were a CPA and Nancy were partner of a CPA firm and similar circumstances were in effect, would your answer change? Do professionals have different duties or higher ethical standards than other businesspeople? Why or why not?

7-2: MORAL CONVICTION AND PROFESSIONAL DUTY

Titus Churchman, CPA, is the newest audit manager in the regional CPA firm of Kant and Ross. Titus is dedicated to the accounting profession and is quite active in the state society. His professional ability is widely recognized not only within his firm but also throughout the city in which he works.

Titus is also a man of strong religious convictions. Among the beliefs that he holds is a strong anti-abortion position. Titus is convinced that upon this issue there is no room for compromise. To that end he is active in Project Alive, a militant pro-life organization that engages in picketing an abortion clinic in the city.

Kant and Ross's largest client is Mega Corporation, a drug company. Many people active in Project Alive have accused Mega of attempting to develop a so-called morning-after pill that would enable a woman to terminate a pregnancy during the first eight weeks at home. Titus has studied the issue and believes that the morning-after pill is a form of abortion. However, Titus does not believe that Mega is engaged in research to develop the morning-after pill. His basis of this belief is that Maggie Sanger, the president of Mega, has emphatically denied that the corporation is engaged in such research. Recently she ordered that this denial be placed in an unaudited section of the company's annual report.

As part of his new duties as partner, Titus is assigned to work directly under Sandra Conner, the partner in charge of the Mega Corporation audit. Titus had never worked on the Mega audit before and he was enthusiastic about the prospect of working for Sandra, for whom he had always held a great deal of respect. The first duty that Sandra assigned to Titus was to review the working papers associated with Mega's research and development account.

During the course of his review Titus was shocked to discover that Mega had indeed secretly committed what he perceived to be a large sum of money toward research on the morning-after pill. Upon further inquiry, Titus learned that chemists at Mega believed they were on the threshold of a dramatic breakthrough in this area. Titus is enraged by this information and is inclined to take his findings to Project Alive. However, upon further reflection he decides to take counsel with Sandra.

Sandra is ambivalent about the issue of abortion. She informs Titus that she believes, first, that the amount of money involved is not material and second, that the representations made by Maggie are in sections of the annual report that are not the responsibility of Kant and Ross. She realizes that Titus is quite sincere in his outrage about the matter and therefore suggests a three-way meeting among Maggie, Titus, and herself.

At the meeting Titus confronts Maggie with his findings. Maggie readily admits that the findings are true. However, she explains that research on the morning-after pill is a closely held corporate secret. This has been necessary for two reasons. First, should a group like Project Alive obtain such information, it could damage Mega Corporation's image in the community. Second, keeping this a secret will enable Mega to obtain a patent on the pill and this will be quite profitable for Mega. Maggie informs Titus that she believes corporate secrets discovered by public auditors should remain secret and that the legal staff of the corporation is prepared to take rigorous action against him and against Kant and Ross should this secret be divulged.

Questions

1. How does the AICPA's Rule 301, Confidential Client Information, treat this case?
2. Can a corporation lie? If so, are there ethical differences between lies told by persons and those told by corporations? If not, how should a moral person respond to lies told by persons on behalf of organizations?
3. Suggest ways that a professional might deal with dilemmas between strongly held personal beliefs and duty to the profession and duty to the client.

NOTES

1. This example is cited in Kenneth Kipnis, *Legal Ethics* (Englewood Cliffs, N.J.: Prentice-Hall, 1986), 41.
2. Michael Davis, "Professionalism Means Putting Your Profession First," *Georgetown Journal of Legal Ethics*, Summer 1988, pp. 341, 346.
3. Milton Friedman, "The Social Responsibility of Business Is to Increase Its Profits," *New York Times Magazine*, September 13, 1970, pp. 32–33, 122–26.
4. Ibid.
5. *Annesley* v. *Angesley*, 17 How. St. Tr. 1140 [Ex. 1743].
6. American Institute of Certified Public Accountants, *Restatement of the Code of Professional Ethics* (AICPA, 1972), p. 12.
7. Ibid.
8. American Institute of Certified Public Accountants, *Code of Professional Conduct*, as amended January 12, 1988, p. 10.
9. Richard W. Stevenson, "Workers Who Turn In Bosses Use Law to Seek Big Rewards, *New York Times*, July 10, 1989, pp. 1, 25.
10. Alasdair MacIntyre, *After Virtue: A Study in Moral Theory* (Notre Dame, Ind.: University of Notre Dame Press, 1981), p. 6.

8

THE ACCOUNTING COMMUNITY: PROFESSIONAL RELATIONSHIPS

Beth Berry had asked the members of the audit team on the Sterns Company audit to meet her for coffee at the office on Saturday morning. There had been the usual good-natured banter at the meeting, but some serious business had also been discussed. Beth believed that she had a good "feel" for how the Sterns' job was going. Moreover, she had been able to hand out assignments for the next phase of the audit.

This job had been a particularly strenuous one. Beth, as partner in charge of the audit, was particularly proud of the group of young professionals she had assembled. As she reflected in her office after the meeting broke up, there had been a great deal of bonding among this group as they were working together on the Sterns' audit. Beth realized that they had actually formed a sort of group or community around this activity. She mused that the accounting profession itself constituted a community—one where members had certain kinds of special relationships and attending responsibilities by virtue of being members of the accounting profession. She wondered what different ethical standards and duties were imposed upon people simply because they had this community relationship. Beth was clearly aware of professional codes of ethics, but she wondered about responsibilities beyond the formal demands of written codes.

Beth knew enough about ethics to realize that relationships among human beings were complex. In fact most, if not all, ethical conflicts arise because of the complexity of these relationships. Once one abandons the option of becoming a hermit, she finds herself in a place where she must relate. People asserting their rights against one another; people fulfilling their duties toward one another—this is the stuff of which ethics is made. Beth thought that since the profession was special, the ethics of the professional must be special also.

PROFESSION AS COMMUNITY

We introduced the notion of profession as community in Chapter 2. The accounting profession constitutes a professional community by its own choice. By its very nature community imposes responsibility upon the membership. Parker Palmer points out that membership in community necessitates that what has an effect upon the whole has an effect upon the individual parts and vice versa. "Community . . . is the nature of reality, the shape of our being. Whether we like it or not, acknowledge it or not, we are in community with one another, implicated in each other's lives."[1] To be in community implies that one cannot divorce himself from the affairs that might affect that community. The implications of this are that each member of the profession is in some measure responsible for the actions of the other members of the profession. In this chapter we explore the implications of profession as community in the realm of ethics.

IMMORALITY

One of the oldest recorded ethical questions is in Genesis: "Am I my brother's keeper?" A modern restatement of this might be: Am I responsible for the actions of other accountants and if so to what degree? The recently published story of Robert P. Clark[2] is instructive. Clark, about whom little is known, is currently being held by authorities in Richmond, Virginia, who believe that he is John E. List, an accountant who allegedly murdered his entire family in New Jersey during 1971 and subsequently disappeared. One fact that is widely known and publicized about Clark is that he is an accountant.

The fact that Mr. Clark is an accountant is potentially harmful to the profession and to all those associated with it in some degree. It is not that any rational person would link murder and accountants because of the act of one accountant. Rather it is that a minute impression has been made on the minds of the public.

In some measure any immoral act of a member of the profession affects the whole because by its very nature the profession has advanced itself to society as a special community deserving special privilege and therefore having special responsibilities. We have tried to create an illusion that is mildly elitist. The public does not expect professional people to commit violent crimes. That is the sort of thing one expects from the laboring "class." So when it happens that professional people also commit violent crimes, the news is somewhat more sensational and pierces the aura that professions attempt to build about themselves.

Therefore, we are our brother's and our sister's keeper. As members of the professional community we cannot escape any chaos associated with that community. We are unable to assume the role of rugged individual in this context. Moral weakness in the community weakens the community defense against its detractors. So the members of the community ought to take action to hold members to high moral and ethical standards. Notice the compartmentalization of professional and personal life does not often work. The linkages between being accountant and whatever else will still occur in the mind of that public from whom we as professionals seek special privilege.

We do, however, run into a particularly sticky wicket when we assume the morality of our peers in the professional community. The question inevitably arises: whose moral standards are to be upheld? Most would agree that accountants would not tolerate murder in our midst (to copy the old West Point code), but what about other acts?

Let's consider adultery. Most accountants would probably say that adultery is immoral. Yet do accountants often get involved in criticizing the private lives of adulterous peers? Many people consider the consumption of alcohol to be immoral. Yet a large number of accountants are not teetotalers. Should accountants who deem drinking to be immoral attempt to alter the behavior of colleagues who imbibe?

The point of this dilemma is that attempting to regulate the morals of others in the community is at best a difficult morass. We will attempt no simplistic solution in this perplexing area except to state that though individual cases must be handled separately, the ethical models of deontologism, utilitarianism, and ethical realism are useful to us. Another ancient rule is also of use here: before we seek to remove a speck from a brother's or a sister's eye, we should seek first to remove the plank from our own eye. In other words, each professional should be more concerned about her own ethical house than that of her professional peers.

KITCHEN TABLING

"Kitchen tabling" may be unique in the public accounting profession. The term is used to describe the behavior of younger members of the profession who work overtime on engagements for clients but fail to report the hours. The clients benefit from this practice since the hours worked are not billed. This practice is widespread among public accounting firms, according to many accountants with whom we have spoken. Yet upper-level managers in these firms—the partners—are adamantly opposed to their younger professional colleagues doing it because of several negative impacts on the firms and ultimately upon the profession.

Why do we find young accounting professionals willing to sacrifice their free time, often under specific instructions and admonitions not to do so, in order to benefit clients? It is surely not out of a sense of altruism. Rather it stems from two sources. First, the competitive pressures in the profession cause middle-level managers (the seniors) to place pressure on the staff to stay within budget on audits. Second, like most upwardly mobile professionals, young CPAs want to look good. Here we find one ethical problem of kitchen tabling—it violates the notion of community since the motive behind it is to benefit self at the expense of others with whom we are in community. We may look at how this occurs from both the deontological and utilitarian perspectives.

From the deontological point of view, kitchen tabling flies in the face of veracity (truth telling) and thus ultimately fidelity (promise keeping). Moreover, the young professional who fails to report the hours she works makes herself look good in comparison with her colleagues who accurately report their hours. This violates another deontological duty, non-maleficence (do no harm). The colleagues of the kitchen tabler suffer harm innocently because she might receive promotion or other reward that they deserve. This promotion or other reward would be based upon deception.

From a utilitarian perspective, the consequences of kitchen tabling are mostly bad for all parties. From the perspective of the partners, the firm does not receive proper compensation for professional services rendered. Moreover, clients who receive services, particularly auditing services, so cheaply, come to expect future prices at comparable bargain levels. Ultimately, clients, the profession, and even society itself suffer as competitive conditions force the quality of audits to deteriorate as kitchen tabling becomes more and more widespread.

Members of the profession, both present and future, also suffer bad consequences from kitchen tabling. Standards for time to complete audit and other work tend to be revised to unrealistic levels as kitchen tabling increases. This puts pressure on other professionals to perform at unrealistic levels and perhaps motivates them to practice kitchen tabling. Thus a vicious circle is created.

Partners of firms are not against kitchen tabling only because of the loss of audit fees. They also lose valuable information on realistic standards for audit work. Thus the information used to put out bids for future services with the same and other clients is distorted.

The kitchen tabler unwittingly creates bad consequences for herself. Having been evaluated at artificially high levels based upon a lie, the professional is expected to perform at these same levels, or even higher ones in the future. Perhaps the only way this can be accomplished is through even more kitchen tabling. So the consequences of kitchen tabling are bad for self, for colleagues, for superiors, for the profession, and for society.

STRESS IN THE ACCOUNTING COMMUNITY

The existence of stress in our present society is well known and well researched.[3] While many decry vocational stress as "bad" for us in terms of personal health and quality of life, we observe that those who succeed in a materialistic society are often those who endure and even thrive on such pressure. As a professional career, accounting is one where the stress demands are particularly onerous. Research among extremely bright and successful accounting professionals reveals that their work weeks *average* from fifty to seventy hours per week.[4]

From the standpoint of ethics, what are the implications of stress? Ethics cannot be reduced to what is "good" or "bad" for one's health or well-being. Unfortunately, a lot of "pop culture" ethics attempts to reduce rightness or wrongness to personal well-being. As Charles Krauthammer puts it: "The way to persuade people to stop doing something is to tell them it is bad for their bods."[5] Yet if we desire to mature from an ethical standpoint, we must go beyond the perspective of self, since the ethically correct course of action may not be the one that maximizes personal gain or pleasure.

Any ethical implications of stress can be examined more intelligently with the use of the ethical models. Either model may be used to attempt to strike a balance between an over-stressed profession and the unreality of a completely "laid back" one. Those who favor a utilitarian approach will want to look at the consequences of different levels of stress. What are the future implications of pathological stress upon the individual accountant, the firm for which he works, the professional community, the business community, and society at large? For example, a CPA laboring under the burden of too much stress could make a bad judgment call on an audit that might in turn cause him to miss a material fraud. The consequences of this would be quite severe to all parties concerned, as many famous audit liability court cases would verify. Again we suggest no simple solution, only the suggestion that those who manage accounting practices analyze the issue intelligently.

As in many ethical situations, the deontological approach provides a way of looking at the issue. Here the emphasis is upon duty. For the professional, duties to the firm and the profession must be balanced against duties to self, family, and the community in which one lives. In popular terms this is known as the balance between personal and professional responsibilities. For managers and owners of accounting practices the issue is between duty to the development of practice and duty to the professional people upon whom, after all, they are building that practice and with whom they are in community by virtue of the notion of profession.

Many will protest that the current stressful environment is forced upon the profession by the competitive environment. Those who employ this argument will state that in order to survive, they must compete as vigorously as the other guy. However, at least some professionals refuse to accept that cop-out. Terry Grear, a CPA in Cincinnati, Ohio, has built his highly successful practice with the underlying principle that the professional people who work for him and their families are more important than the practice of Grear & Company. According to employees of his firm who were interviewed with the promise of confidentiality, Grear backs up his policies by personal example and by personally insisting that his personnel not overwork. Grear even runs seminars for clients on how to run a successful business using his principles. The atmosphere around his office is remarkably different from that found in most CPA firms. From a utilitarian standpoint the consequences of Grear's policies are mostly good for working conditions. From a deontological standpoint, Grear adheres to the Kantian advice to treat persons as ends rather than means to an end.[6]

FAMILY TIES

As we look at the accounting profession as a community, we must be cognizant of another community that is much older and has its own set of complex relationships. We refer to the family. Our interest here concerns only potential conflicts between ties of family and ties of professional community.

Problems are not unusual in any business organization where blood ties exist. Serious personnel problems especially occur when the boss's son or daughter is hired and put into a position over a more experienced employee. Alternatively, that same son or daughter might receive a promotion instead of a more qualified employee. Even if the slighted employee is not in fact more qualified, the fact of the blood relationship between boss and child may very well cause problems from the appearance perspective. These kinds of issues in a business or professional setting generally come under the rubric "nepotism."

The abuse of nepotism would seem to be particularly obnoxious in the context of a professional community. After all, the profession is a group of people committed to the practice of accounting and dedicated to service to clients and to society. In this context special favor to a family member, especially an undeserving one, appears to be out of line. For example, should a son or daughter be admitted to partnership and placed in charge of a prestigious audit simply by virtue of blood ties? Such action is potentially harmful to colleagues who are not rewarded for their merit, to clients who do not receive the best service available, and to society, which suffers potential harm from inadequacy in accounting practice.

Yet in public accounting, bringing family members into the practice is extremely common. This is especially true in the case of small practitioners and small partnerships. We stress that running a family business in itself is not unethical. One of the largest international accounting firms was founded by two brothers as Ernst and Ernst. Interestingly, that firm, now Ernst and Young, is known for having one of the strongest anti-nepotism policies in the industry.

Large public accounting firms are more restrictive with respect to nepotism than their small counterparts. At the Big Six firms, the rules about nepotism vary. Some will not allow a relative to work anywhere for the firm, while others permit relatives but only at offices in separate geographical locations.

Ethical problems might also occur when relatives work for clients. Here questions of independence arise (see Chapter 3). In any particular location the business community is a complex web. The professional accounting community interacts with and is in fact a part of this larger business community. We might reasonably expect members of the same family to be employed by firms and their clients. While direct and material indirect financial interests are clearly prohibited by the code of conduct, the place to draw the line, especially for independence in appearance, is not clear.

In our changing culture, where women are becoming increasingly successful in and important to the profession, we find that family ties can be created quickly by way of marriage. We will cover the complex area of dating and marriage more fully in Chapter 9. Here we simply point out that in today's business community, family relationships are formed and broken more quickly than in days gone by. Thus ethical questions arising because of family ties are in a fluid state. For example, if a CPA marries a woman whose grown daughter is an employee of a client, need we be concerned from the standpoint of independence?

Ethical issues with respect to family ties are far too complex to be resolved by simple rules. Consider the fact that in some families a mother and son may have no personal relationship whatsoever and therefore ethical questions are unlikely to arise (except for questions of independence in appearance questions). In another family the informal dynamics might be such that distant second cousins are thick as thieves. No independence in appearance questions would arise here. Yet a very real issue of independence in fact could exist. The same logic may be applied to possibilities of unethical nepotism. In any event, the ethical agent is responsible to judge each case on its own merits.

FORMERLY PROHIBITED ACTS

The sense of community that we have in the accounting profession, and more particularly in the community of public accountants, was once much stronger than it is today. This assertion is supported by a look back at former codes of professional ethics of the AICPA. A major section of the *Restatement of the Code of Professional Ethics* concerned responsibilities to colleagues.[7] Today's *Code of Professional Conduct* is virtually silent on this subject.[8]

What are these ethical responsibilities that were once important enough to be encoded? They were prohibitions against encroachment—that is, attempting to take another's client and prohibitions against offering employment to employees of another CPA without first informing that CPA (Rules 401 and 402).[9] Today's code has replaced these ethical rules with the stark statement, "there are currently no rules in the 400 series."[10] This states in effect that there are currently no rules governing responsibilities toward colleagues.

Comparing the two codes, the reader will find two other major differences. Under "Other Responsibilities and Practices," the old code forbade solicitation and advertising and contained a rule against incompatible occupations (Rules 502 and 504).[11] The new code prohibits only false, misleading, or deceptive advertising. It is silent about incompatible occupations.[12]

These differences in the codes are more than simple rule changes. They describe the different atmosphere today in the professional accounting community as compared with a decade and a half ago. It is instructive to read in the former code about the responsibilities to colleagues that once were and no longer are part of the ethos of the profession because of the strong flavor of community that comes through: "The support of a profession by its members and their cooperation with one another are essential elements of professional character. The public confidence and respect which a CPA enjoys is largely the result of the cumulative accomplishments of all CPAs, past and present."[13]

The current *Code of Professional Conduct* avoids this kind of language. What is it about the community of public accountants that causes them to abandon what was once so strongly entrenched in their culture? Many assert that the profession was forced by the regulatory officials of the Federal Trade Commission and by decisions of the federal courts to abandon practices once deemed part of professional ethics and now considered illegal restraints of trade.

Admittedly, the immediate reason public accountants changed their code of ethics can be traced to changes in the law and perhaps changes in the public's perception of what constitutes acceptable professional behavior. Yet the interesting question arises: Were these practices really part of ethical behavior among professional people or cleverly disguised means to protect a guild?[14] Perhaps the answer to this question can never truly be known. Yet many thoughtful people are saddened by the current competitive practices of professional CPAs, which resemble more the behavior of aggressive capitalist robber barons than that of a community of people dedicated to practicing a profession.

AFFIRMATIVE ACTION

Who will become members of the professional community? Clearly, only persons well trained, competent, and interested in a career as an accountant will be likely candidates for membership in the community. In the past another qualification would have been listed among the requirements for acceptance in the professions. Historically, all professions were the preserves of white males. But, through social pressures, individual challenges, legislative actions, and court decisions (at the state and federal levels), old barriers were torn down. Now affirmative action in employment is a fact of life.

Affirmative action is a controversial idea. It has sometimes been criticized as "reverse discrimination." It does, by definition, require programs designed to equalize hiring and promotion opportunities for groups who have been historically disadvantaged. Proponents of affirmative action believe that past biases based on race, national origin, gender, or handicap have made it necessary to take affirmative steps to increase the numbers of members of such groups in firms and corporations.

The Supreme Court has shifted frequently in its interpretation of the laws—municipal, state, and federal—that require affirmative action in public settings.[15] On the other hand, private corporations (and educational institutions) have nearly all agreed that diversity of personnel is a noble goal; hiring policies have tended to reflect that commitment. Nevertheless, it is still evident that the effects of racial and gender discrimination continue.

There are a variety of ethical issues in the realm of affirmative action. Rigid formulas or quotas are controversial; hiring goals are less so. Yet the fundamental reservations about affirmative action, according to Bill Shaw, may be reduced to four:

1. It is race conscious rather than color-blind
2. It benefits individuals because of group identity
3. It presents an unfair burden on the present generations of white workers
4. It demeans the real achievements of women and minorities[16]

All of these criticisms can be debated or rebutted. What is clear is that our society remains both divided about affirmative action and generally in favor of some form of racial and gender equality. Therefore, countering discrimination often becomes a matter of individual conscience and community discussion. Despite the fact that the accounting profession has certainly begun to acknowledge the need to discuss the nuances of racial and gender equality, it is not without its critics. In August 1989 a coalition of minority business groups and civil rights organizations filed petitions with both the Department of Justice and the Federal Trade Commission seeking to stop mergers between the nation's largest accounting firms. In these documents the Big Eight was described as "the nation's largest and most powerful all-white semi-secret society."[17]

The ethical question we need to address is not whether or not members of minority groups should be hired as accountants. The accounting profession along with the rest of American society long ago settled the ethical question of excluding persons from the professional community because of race, religion, or culture. The question concerns upward mobility of these accountants once they are in the profession. We assert that it is not only good ethics, it is also good business to include persons from diverse backgrounds in our profession. This is especially true in the case of large international accounting firms that find themselves doing business in places where cultural diversity is an asset from a human resource and client development point of view.

Because we accept people from different races, religions, and cultures as members of the professional community, it is important that we include them in the professional community. Inclusion means among other things that these accountants can rise to the level of partner in public accounting and to the highest level of management in corporations. Our accounting community exists because of the practice of the art of accounting. Differences that may separate us as professionals should be laid aside because that is the right thing to do and because by doing so we assure good consequences.

Because of the community nature of the profession, accountants should be aggressive in ensuring that intolerance of their peers is not condoned. This can be accomplished both negatively and positively. For example, clubs that practice racial exclusion should be shunned by professionals who count members of that race among their peers.[18] On the positive side, efforts at socializing and personal acceptance make a greater statement than words alone can.

Although room for improvement still exists, the profession in public as well as private accounting has made great strides in this area. The same remarks may easily be made about gender difference in the professional community. However, this subject's complexity will be discussed in the next chapter.

CONCLUSION

By its very nature as a community, the accounting profession contains dynamic and living relationships. In turn, these human relationships inevitably lead to ethical conflicts and to ethical dilemmas. In this chapter we have discussed several of these kinds of problems as they are found in the accounting profession.

Human relationships are complex; so too are the ethical conflicts and dilemmas that arise from these relationships. No simple solution can be proposed for any class of ethical conflict. Each must be judged and analyzed on its own merits. The ethical models suggested in this book are useful to the professional accountant faced with such conflicts as both a rational ethical agent and as a member of the professional community.

CASE STUDIES

8-1: MORALITY AND PROFESSIONAL RELATIONS

Patricia Land and Robert Welsh have been friendly rivals since their student days at Knozit University. They were both members of Beta Alpha Psi and had run against each other for president. Upon graduation this had continued as each had passed the CPA exam on the first try.

They accepted employment at rival regional CPA firms in the same city. Each was admitted to partnership this year. Over the years they had maintained friendly banter about their successes and failures.

Recently Robert had succeeded in what he considered a real coup. One of Patricia's major clients, Bogan Meat Packers, had switched to Robert's firm. What pleased Robert most particularly about this switch was that Patricia had been the partner in charge of the Bogan audit and today he had been named the new partner in charge of that audit for his firm.

Robert has decided to celebrate his victory by asking Patricia to join him for dinner. Patricia knows she is in for some needling but accepts, as she feels her turn will come again.

On the way to dinner Robert recalls some papers he needs to take downtown. He and Patricia stop by his home to get them. While Robert is looking for the papers, Patricia opens an end table drawer looking for matches and discovers within it some hard-core pornography.

Patricia is surprised at her discovery, since she did not know Robert read this type of material. She recalls that Jerry Springwell, the president at Bogan, is a man of strong fundamentalist religious views who is an active supporter of the anti-pornography campaign in the city. She suspects Mr. Springwell would not want his books audited by someone who indulges in pornography.

Questions

1. In the current competitive environment of public accounting, should Patricia let Mr. Springwell know of her discovery?
2. Suppose the facts are the same except Patricia and Robert work for the same firm and are the two top candidates for partner in charge of the office in the city. Assume further that Mr. Springwell is a regional partner who will influence the promotion decision, instead of president of Bogan. Does this change your answer?
3. If Patricia discovered under similar circumstances that Robert was not a consumer but a producer and distributor of hard-core pornography, would this change your answer to question 1 or 2? Why or why not?
4. Suppose Patricia strongly objects to pornography on moral grounds. Does this change the answers to questions 1, 2, or 3? Why or why not?

8-2: FAMILY TIES

John Meadows, CPA, is a partner in charge of the audit of the Community of the Redeemed Hospital. From his point of view things are progressing well on this engagement. The manager of the audit has drawn up the audit report and is recommending an unqualified opinion. John has reviewed the working papers and is inclined to agree.

At the same time Lin Turner, of the MAS staff, has been assisting the hospital in choosing a computer system that will enable the hospital to network all accounting functions. John is somewhat surprised that the company chose a system from a new, unknown computer company, Rambutan, over large, better-known competitors. When John asked Lin about this she told him the system offered by Rambutan was faster, more reliable, and less expensive than those offered by the larger competitors. Besides, Lin assured John that while she had worked daily with the hospital project, the decision had been made by hospital management.

John decides that he wants one more look at the working papers before he signs the audit report. He feels he can finish his review in the morning. That night he has the following conversation with his wife, Vicki:

Vicki: I had lunch with Daddy today. He is on top of the world.

John: Why's that?

Vicki: Community of the Redeemed Hospital has decided to install a Rambutan computer system.

John: Why would that make your father happy?

Vicki: Oh, honey, don't you know? Daddy is the head of a venture capital partnership which has provided ninety percent of Rambutan's financing. Daddy has poured half of his life savings into this project. The decision made by Community of the Redeemed will make Daddy a very wealthy man.

John: I had no idea your father was head of a venture capital partnership.

Vicki: That's because you never listen. By the way, Daddy sure appreciated working with Lin Turner. He told her he just knew you would be pleased if the decision went Rambutan's way.

Questions

1. Should John allow the information he has learned from Vicki influence his actions with respect to the audit report? Why or why not?

2. From a deontological perspective, will John do anything wrong if he issues an unqualified opinion on Community of the Redeemed Hospital? From a utilitarian perspective? Discuss without reference to any AICPA rules on the matter. Do AICPA rules change your answer?

NOTES

1. P. J. Palmer, *To Know As We Are Known* (New York: Harper and Row, 1983), p. 122.
2. C. D. May, "Prosaic Life of Suspect in '71 New Jersey Murders," *New York Times,* June 9, 1989, pp. B1, B4.
3. See, for example, C. Hymowitz, "Stepping Off the Fast Track," *Wall Street Journal,* June 13, 1989, p. B1.
4. P. G. Cottell and C. M. Michael, "Support Relationships and Women in Public Accounting," Unpublished working paper at Miami University, 1990.
5. C. Krauthammer, "Our Loss of Moral Perspective," *Cincinnati Enquirer,* January 18, 1988, p. A-10. Krauthammer carries this theme further in "An Unending Quest for Self-Love," *Cincinnati Enquirer,* May 7, 1989, p. E-3.
6. This information is based upon interviews conducted by P. G. Cottell.
7. American Institute of Certified Public Accountants, *Restatement of the Code of Professional Ethics,* 1972, pp. 13–14, 23–24.
8. American Institute of Certified Public Accountants, *Code of Professional Conduct,* as amended January 12, 1988.
9. AICPA, 1972.
10. AICPA, 1988, p. 12.
11. AICPA, 1972.
12. AICPA, 1988.
13. AICPA, 1972, p.13.
14. In *The Rise of Professionalism,* M. S. Larson argues that economic self-interest is the primary motivating force behind the entire notion of professionalism.
15. C. D. Ransic, "The Supreme Court and Affirmative Action: An Evolving Standard or Compounded Confusion?" *Employee Relations Law Journal,* Autumn 1988, pp. 175–90.
16. B. Shaw, "Affirmative Action: An Ethical Evaluation," *Journal of Business Ethics,* October 1988, pp. 763–70.
17. K. Rankin, "Minority Coalition Attacks Big Mergers," *Accounting Today,* August 28, 1989, pp. 1, 17.
18. The excuse "I have no peers who are members of an excluded race," is not a valid one since the profession asserts that it claims to be open to all races.

9

MEN AND WOMEN—BOYS AND GIRLS: ROLES AND RESPONSIBILITIES

The two college professors could see the look of pain as Liz, a young accountant, looked up from her desk in response to the question that she had been asked during the interview. "It's hard to explain," she said slowly. "I know all the guys around the office will tell you that men and women are treated equally around here. Plus, they probably have data to back it up. But, yes, I have to work harder to get ahead here because I'm a woman. I can't prove it; I just know it in my 'knower.' " Remarks similar to these were heard on several occasions during the course of a research project on women in public accounting.[1] The women who made these remarks were highly successful people on the fast track in large international accounting firms. Moreover, a few of their male colleagues concurred.

Women have been rapidly entering the profession during the last decade and a half. The expansion of opportunities into what was one of the last male bastions to fall has progressed to the point where over 50 percent of new hires are female in many firms. Brenda T. Acken, who chaired the recent AICPA special committee to examine upward mobility of women in accounting, asserts that within twenty years women are expected to constitute 50 percent of the profession.[2] The presence of women in the profession has created new ethical dilemmas: issues of equality, issues of upward mobility, issues of propriety, and issues of morality. We examine some of these sometimes emotionally laden issues in this chapter.

ISSUES OF EQUALITY

Irrespective of one's beliefs about women's issues or equality of the sexes, one point is clear: by virtue of the fact that a person is in the profession, she is a member of the professional community. Therefore, the treatment that person receives and the role that person plays must be evaluated within the context of community and the inherent meaning of community membership. As an example consider that the former code of ethics of the AICPA called "professional courtesy" an "obligation" and that it admonished its members "to deal with fellow practitioners in a manner which will not detract from their reputation and well-being."[3] From a deontological perspective we may view these as duties owed by members of the community to one another. From a utilitarian point of view we may postulate the consequences that unethical treatment might have upon other members of the community and ultimately upon the profession as a whole.

Duty

In Chapter 2 we discussed professionalism and the fact that accountants who practice public accounting loudly proclaim and universally believe that their vocation is a profession. We also discussed the current movements by accountants who are not in the realm of public accounting to actively seek professional status and recognition. Many believe these accountants have achieved this sought-after status. Therefore it follows that one who is an accountant should conduct herself as a professional.

In Chapter 8 we addressed many of the duties that professionals owe to one another and to the profession as a whole. The question we address here is whether duties owed by or duties owed to professionals change by virtue of the fact that the professional is female. In the absence of some logical reason to the contrary, the answer to this question would have to be no. In the United States and increasingly in other cultures, equality of women in the workplace is at least given lip service. One would presume that "the workplace" would include the professional workplace.

Therefore professional duties are owed to and by all members of the professional community. Yet it is not enough to give assent to this notion; we professionals must act upon it. Professional people should have the opportunity to advance in the profession based upon their professional qualifications and contributions to the firm and to the profession. Professional people should respect one another as persons—as peers in the community. These are lofty goals, but surely they do not change because of the gender of the community member. As Kant stated, each rational person should be treated as an end and not as a means to an end.[4] By virtue of their admission to the profession women have the right to expect treatment as professionals and have assumed the duty to treat other professionals in a like manner.

Let's say for example that a client has invited Fred to a lunch where some important strategic planning discussions will take place. The client asks Fred to bring "a couple of more" professionals with him. Fred believes that this meeting will have an important career impact upon the people he brings because it will afford them the opportunity to participate in high-level discussions and they will get hands-on experience of the kinds of activity it takes to build a client base.

In Fred's opinion his two most talented and dedicated subordinates are Beth and Bob. He therefore decides that they should attend. Later Fred finds out that the client has scheduled the lunch at a private club in the city with a "men only" policy. So Fred invites John to come to the meeting in the place of Beth.

In this case, Fred has violated a professional duty toward Beth. Beth, through no fault of her own, is being denied an opportunity that she deserves. This violates a fundamental duty of justice. Fred should have asked the client to schedule the meeting for another place, explaining that Beth was the most qualified person for the engagement.

Consequences

Utilitarian ethics support the notion of equality of the sexes in the profession. We need not go to metaphysical utilitarian goals to demonstrate this. The most bare knuckles kind of consequential thinking reveals it. Simply stated, the accounting profession needs women. There is intense and increasing demand for trained and intelligent people in the accountant profession. Women meet a great deal of this demand.

If bright and motivated women are treated unfairly or even if they believe this to be the case, they will take their talents elsewhere. The consequences to the profession would be a severe shortage of qualified people. Therefore treating women as professional peers is not only good ethics; it is also good business.

One final detrimental consequence can accrue to the accounting profession if women in the accounting community are treated unfairly. This is the erosion of the public's perception of the accounting community as a profession. As we stated in Chapter 2, one of the most important factors in maintaining the benefits of professionalism is that society must recognize the professional status of the group wishing to attain or to maintain professional status. As long as society favors basic fairness and justice toward women in the workplace—and we believe that it does—any profession that treats its female members unfairly or unjustly will do so at its peril.

ISSUES OF UPWARD MOBILITY

Brenda T. Acken expresses well the issue of career advancement opportunities for women in our profession.

> Admission to partnership is affected by many considerations, notably technical, management, client relationship and practice development abilities. There is no question about women's technical ability, but traditional beliefs and attitudes regarding other abilities raise questions. For example, are women at a competitive disadvantage in comparison to men in obtaining new audit clients and maintaining existing ones? Is there a women's "network?" Moreover, some partners may believe that men are generally more dedicated than women to a professional career.[5]

One important measure of whether or not women are receiving fair treatment in the profession is evidence of their being promoted and compensated for their professional services. The AICPA in recognition of this fact recently appointed a special committee to examine two issues: (1) that although many women have risen to senior levels in accounting firms, relatively few have been admitted to partnership and (2) that many accountants believe admission to partnership is more difficult for women than for men. The report of the Special Committee on Upward Mobility of Women was published in March 1988.[6]

The mere fact that the issues identified by the AICPA are true does not present an ethical problem per se. In order to discern the ethical concerns involved in the upward mobility of women, the reasons for barriers to partnership must be discovered. Three possible reasons are: first, that the cycle is not complete; second, that women leave the profession before being promoted to partner; and third, that because of gender bias women face barriers to partnership.

By stating that the cycle is not complete, we refer to an often expressed belief that women simply have not been in the profession long enough to be promoted to the partner level. Because women began to enter the profession in significant numbers about fifteen years ago and it takes about twelve to fifteen years to be promoted to partner, this argument currently has validity. However, as time passes it will no longer hold water. This reason does not present ethical problems by itself.

The other two reasons will not be cured simply by the passage of time. In these two we find issues and dilemmas of interest from an ethical standpoint. We shall therefore focus attention upon the validity of these issues.

The AICPA special committee believes that the factors that affect upward mobility of women are not unique to the accounting profession, but rather are universal obstacles confronting women in the general workplace. However, Cottell and Michael found that while women in the profession encounter many of the same problems faced by their peers in other business situations, public accounting presents several unique aspects.

Why Women Leave

The factors that cause women to leave the profession are entangled with the very same factors that cause barriers to upward mobility for those who do stay in the profession. They can be classified into two broad areas: the balance of personal and professional responsibilities, and real or perceived biases that impede the upward mobility of women in accounting.

The balance of personal and professional responsibilities issue is a particularly thorny one in public accounting. In this profession, working hours are not predictable. Clients see CPAs as continuous service providers who should be available when they are needed. This places tremendous burdens upon female professionals, because in most families the woman is the primary manager, according to the AICPA Special Committee.[7] Moreover, family is generally of greater concern to women than to men.

This problem is magnified by a subtle attitude in the business community. Marriage tends to be viewed as an asset for the male executive but a hindrance for the female executive. A wife is a helper who will allow the man to focus more attention toward his business life. For the woman marriage implies that she will have additional responsibilities that will divert her attention from her career responsibilities.

The issue has led some companies and some accounting firms to experiment with what is coming to be known as "the Mommy track." Proponents of this management style suggest that women have the option of a slower career path to partner than the traditional one. The idea is to permit a smaller client load, to allow for flexibility in hours, or to devise other means to help professional women cope with the balance of personal and professional responsibilities.

Women who desire to be on the Mommy track would self-select. In return for the reduced load of clients or hours, they would know that the time to be promoted to partner would be longer. Presumably the option of this alternate track would also be available to men.

The Mommy track issue is controversial and some of the controversy contains ethical overtones. Critics state that the Mommy track will relegate women in the workplace to second-class citizen status.

Moreover, such a policy flies in the face of the American ideal to promote whoever is best qualified and has earned the promotion with hard work. In short, the Mommy track raises the issue of justice for both the person on this career path and for those who are not on the alternate track but are competing for the scarce partner positions. Nevertheless, women interviewed by Cottell and Michael tended to favor at least having the option of an alternate career path. One professional women was actually on a half-time basis with her firm and was quite pleased with the arrangement.

Women also leave public accounting because of real or perceived barriers to their upward mobility. In other words, some women leave the profession because they believe—rightly or wrongly—that opportunities for advancement are better for women in careers outside public accounting. Here the issue becomes entangled with the idea that women are not promoted because of their gender. We are unable to discern the difference between women not being promoted to partner because of gender and their leaving because they "see the handwriting on the wall." This is particularly true in large public accounting firms that have an "up or out" policy under which one either is promoted or is politely asked to leave the firm.

Gender-Based Barriers

The AICPA special committee and the research of Cottell and Michael revealed several biases women in accounting face. Some are quite subtle. Blatant and obvious discrimination is no longer evident for the most part. More deeply held attitudes and beliefs of both men and women are where we find the ethical issues in today's professional environment.

One gender-specific barrier cited by the AICPA special committee is that women are less aware than men of success criteria in accounting such as visibility within the organization, the benefits of a mentor, and the importance of presenting a successful self-image. Specifically, the committee claims that female professionals think good performance is enough for career advancement. Women also believe that hard work will enable them to overcome any barriers that they might encounter, according to the committee.

Interestingly, the women interviewed by Cottell and Michael did not confirm the findings of the AICPA special committee. Most of these women were aware of success criteria at their firms and did not feel that good performance alone would enable them to get ahead. They realized that they had to do more than work hard to reach their career goals but felt they were unable to engage in some of the forms of office politics necessary for success. Of course, this was a source of frustration to them.

The AICPA special committee stated that women need to learn the importance of working as a team. Some social scientists believe that women have deficiencies in this area because they lack opportunity to participate in team sports. On the other hand, some feminists state that women are by nature better team members because they tend to be conciliators. The jury is still out on this issue.

The AICPA special committee also stated that women receive less advice from their superiors about how to succeed in an organization than their male counterparts. This appears at all three levels of supporting relationships (see Chapter 5). The committee believes women need increased mentoring opportunities in accounting.

Women face cultural attitudes that can affect their ability to advance in their careers. Many people view women as wives, mothers, and daughters rather than business colleagues. These attitudes are detrimental to women if held by colleagues but devastating if held by clients, since advancement to partner depends primarily upon the ability to build and hold a client base.

As seemingly harmless a matter as the game of golf can cause grief to women in public accounting. Many CPAs use golf to enhance relationships with their clients. However, this is an avenue almost closed to women in the profession. One woman interviewed by Cottell and Michael explained that many men do not like women on the golf course. They feel women slow down the game and lessen the competition. On the other hand, if the woman is an accomplished golfer, they resent being beaten by a woman! This particular woman, who was good at the game, found herself holding back so that she did not commit the sin of winning.

Another cultural attitude concerns personal deportment. Outward expressions of anger and blatant displays of aggressiveness are not only tolerated in men but even admired by some people. For women, on the other hand, such behavior is viewed as either feminine weakness or unfeminine behavior. This issue was recently aired in the court suit between Price Waterhouse and Ann Hopkins, a manager who, despite bringing in considerable business to her firm and billing more hours than any other candidate, had failed to make partner. Written evaluations from firm partners branded her "'macho,' foulmouthed and harsh to co-workers." One partner suggested that she learn "to walk, talk and dress 'more femininely . . . wear makeup, have her hair styled and wear jewelry.'" In this instance the court upheld lower court rulings that Hopkins had been discriminated against.[8]

A basic issue needs to be resolved with respect to cultural attitudes about women. Should women change? Should they exhibit the kinds of behavior that have been the keys to success for men in the business and professional community? Many have suggested this course of action and have even suggested that the change begin at the child-rearing stage, where boys and girls should be treated more alike.

The other argument states that women are after all basically different from men. Recent research has added evidence to this view.[9] Feminists have begun to adopt this view and state that society and its attitudes need the changing. The business and professional community should recognize, value, and reward those unique attributes that women bring to the workplace by virtue of their femininity. From a community perspective the profession would be expanded and enhanced were it able to embrace this attitude. However, it remains to be seen whether the rigors of the current competitive environment would allow such a change to take root.

Women in accounting encounter stress in the same way as their male counterparts (see Chapter 8). The AICPA special committee believes that the problem of stress is greater for women than for men. The reason for this is found in the factors we have mentioned previously. Women feel a greater burden under the balance of personal and professional responsibilities. Women face cultural discrimination. Women perceive that they must perform better than men in order to get ahead. All these things aggravate the stressful environment in public accounting. Thus while everyone in public accounting must face long hours and the stress that goes along with them, women are less tolerant of them. Hence they leave the profession.

The AICPA special committee found that some organizations do not recognize the problems encountered by women. On the other hand, most of the people interviewed by Cottell and Michael—many of whom were at the highest levels of their firms—were not only aware of, but were actively seeking, solutions to the problems faced by women in the profession. Some of the ongoing policy changes discovered in this research included cafeteria-style benefit packages, in-house day care programs, flexible hours, and attempts at formal "mentoring" systems. Several of the partners and managers interviewed stated that the primary gender-specific problems female accountants faced were due to clients upon whom the profession and the professional must ultimately depend.

Earlier in this chapter we discussed how both deontological and utilitarian ethical models support the ideal of equality for women in the profession. It follows that if women are treated as equal to men in the professional community then they will have equal opportunity for advancement. For the profession to remain a healthy, ethical community, it must forthrightly face the issue of upward mobility for women in real terms. Happily, our profession is continuing to make progress in this area. The AICPA's special committee report contains guidance—both for professional women and for employers of professional women—that has a great deal of merit.[10]

ISSUES OF PROPRIETY

Propriety refers to standards that are "socially acceptable" in conduct or speech. Of course the first question that might be asked is "acceptable to whom?" In our context we speak of acceptable to the community of professionals. In this chapter we will speak of propriety with respect to the conduct of men and women in the profession. Ethical implications are embedded in this issue.

Office Romance

Lisa A. Mainiero has recently published the results of research on dating, sexual relations, and marriage in the workplace.[11] She is surprisingly supportive of such relationships. "Attractions at work are a natural part of the conviviality of daily office life. They should not be spurned or dismissed as inconsequential. One of the consequences of the new sexual revolution is that men and women will meet, marry, and fall in love on the job. It is unrealistic to think otherwise."[12]

Are ethical issues raised by the occurrence of office romance? While dating and marriage relationships seem strictly personal, they can have ethical implications in two areas addressed earlier in the book.

The first issue is independence (see Chapter 3). Is it within the standards of the profession for a professional to date the employee of a client? We encounter the same ethical issues here as in any client-CPA relationship—independence in fact and independence in appearance.

With respect to independence in fact we must admit that dating relationships may be emotionally charged. In many cases judgment may be clouded. This includes professional judgment. With respect to independence in appearance the issue is particularly murky, since here we speak of independence in the eye of the beholder.

Dating relationships or affairs have the potential to be problematic for the professional. Should such relationships lead to marriage, the questions about independence become even more pronounced. As more and more women come into the business community and as they rise to higher levels in both accounting and client firms, the questions of independence can become more serious. The profession does not have clear guidelines in this area. More thoughtful discussion and consideration are necessary.

The second issue is very much akin to the nepotism issue discussed in Chapter 8. Both public accounting firms and other organizations are much more tolerant of office romance than they used to be. Public accounting firms are less tolerant than many other organizations should these relationships lead to marriage, according to Mainiero. She reports that two Big Six firms, Arthur Andersen and Price Waterhouse, strictly prohibit partners from marrying other employees.[13]

Sexual Static

Sexual static is found when actions in the business community taken for purely business reasons are sometimes misinterpreted by the opposite sex.[14] For example, a male CPA might invite a female colleague to dinner in order to discuss an upcoming audit engagement and she might wrongly interpret this as an unwelcome initiation of romance and thus decline the invitation. Accountants of both sexes are likely to encounter this in any organization. Yet for the female professional in public accounting, the problem can be particularly perplexing with respect to clients.

The building and maintenance of a client base seems to create most of the problem. A common means of maintaining client relationships for the male CPA is to ask a client to dinner and perhaps some socializing afterward. Suppose the CPA is instead an attractive woman in her thirties who asks the client, a married man in his fifties, out to such an evening. Her motives are purely business in nature, but how does the client interpret it? Also, how does that client's wife interpret it? Many women in public accounting believe that this sort of dynamic creates a competitive disadvantage for them.

Cultural attitudes and sexual static can also cause other problems for women in accounting. Accounting, both public and private, is a career that requires the accountant to be gone from the family overnight. Some people believe it is not appropriate for a woman to be away from her family overnight. If the one who holds this belief is a client (for the CPA) or someone high in the organization (for any accountant), a real problem is created for the professional woman.

Sexual static may also cause problems among colleagues. For example, one female accountant we know is a college professor. She relates that no one even takes notice if two men from the otherwise all-male department go to lunch together. Yet if she goes to lunch with a male colleague, remarks are often heard. These remarks might be made in jest, but they are not funny because they cause pain. Here we have a violation of the duty of non-maleficence caused by sexual static and entrenched cultural attitudes.

ISSUES OF MORALITY

We promised a book not on morality but on practical ethics. Nevertheless, in the realm of men and women in the profession, two ethical issues that arise also have clear moral implications—sexual harassment and certain kinds of office romance. We shall address each briefly.

Sexual Harassment

Sexual harassment is an annoying or unwelcome sexual advance or imposition made with the suggestion that inappropriate rewards or penalties will result from compliance or refusal to comply. Most often women are harassed by men who exert some power over them, usually in a job situation. There are occasions where women harass men, and either men or women may be sexually harassed by another person of the same sex. Sexual harassment may also come from co-workers. Women in traditionally male fields are sometimes systematically harassed by their male peers in an effort to drive them away. People who, because they are the sole support of themselves or their families, need their jobs most desperately may be singled out for sexual harassment because they fear losing their pay.

Sexual harassment is not only unethical, it is illegal. By today's standards sexual harassment is so universally condemned that one would not think it worthy of ethical discussion. Yet the phenomenon occurs even among professional people. We suggest that sexual harassment is particularly abhorrent in the context of a profession. Such conduct strikes at the very heart of the notion of a community of people who respect one another.

The unwanted advance need not be overt to constitute unprofessional behavior. One woman interviewed by Cottell and Michael related that a partner of a firm had the habit of patting her on the head—something he did not do to her male peers. She asked him not to do it any more, and when it occurred again she left that firm. Here we see a case where the ethical principle of justice was violated. The victim of the harassment left the firm while the perpetrator remained as a member in good standing.

In the final analysis all members of the professional community are victims when sexual harassment occurs. People who are plagued by sexual harassment suffer from tension, frustration, anxiety, and above all anger. As a result they either leave the profession or are unable to function properly if they remain. The community is thus deprived of a valued member and the perpetrator who is left unchallenged is free to seek another person to harass.

Office Romance Revisited

In Chapter 8 we asked whether we in the professional community have higher ethical standards than society as a whole and, if so, how are we to determine what those standards are. One striking aspect of Mainiero's book is the ethical decision model she repeats throughout the work. That model is hedonistic utilitarianism. Simply stated, Mainiero's advice to her readers is that they should weigh the pleasure they derive from an office romance with the possible consequences—good or bad—that the relationship might have for their career success.

Hedonistic utilitarianism is not an ethical model that thinking people take very seriously any more. The ethics of office romance should involve things other than personal pleasure and career success. The profession is a community, after all, and its ethics should rise to a higher plane. We suggest that either the wider consequences of office romance or the rightness or wrongness of such a relationship be taken into account in each individual case. Some office romances are for any number of reasons not within the ethical limits and standards of the accounting profession. For example, an adulterous office romance raises questions of promise keeping and questions of its effects upon families. Exploitative office romance raises questions of non-maleficence and the consequences of promotion for other than reasons of merit, which in turn violates the principle of justice.

Mainiero, who overall seems to favor office romance, gives stern warning against office romance situations where the relationship is between boss and subordinate or mentor and protégé. Two dangers exist in such relationships. First, while the relationship is going on other professionals in the office may resent special treatment they perceive the subordinate is receiving—again the issue of justice is raised. Second, such relationships sometimes turn into sexual harassment cases when the subordinate or protégé desires to end the relationship and the other party desires to continue it.

CONCLUSION

We entitled our chapter "Men and Women—Boys and Girls" for a reason. Professional behavior calls for the members of the accounting community to conduct themselves as mature adults in their relationships with one another. Ethical behavior will most likely emerge when professional relationships are based upon respect for one another as persons—persons in pursuit of excellence in the profession.

The presence of women in the accounting profession has enhanced and enriched the accounting community as a whole. This change in the profession has given accountants the historic opportunity to reexamine the ethics involved with the relationships of men and women. The profession, by making an honest appraisal of these matters, will proceed into the next era stronger for its efforts.

CASE STUDIES

9-1: OFFICE ROMANCE

The stakes were high on the SEC filing for the Fortune 500 company located on the West Coast. Therefore Phil decided to send two of his most dynamic and expert partners from New York out to Los Angeles to consult with management. Steve and Janie had never worked together before. In fact, they hardly knew each other. However, they hit it off right away.

During the long cross-country plane trip they worked on some last-minute planning of the technical aspect of this job. It was a high stakes and high pressure assignment. Yet both of these young professionals were tried and tested and actually thrived on this sort of work.

In the weeks that followed, the days were long and filled with stress. Both the management of the company and the professional accountants were impressed with the quality of the work accomplished by Steve and Janie. After others had returned to their homes, Steve and Janie would often linger to polish and review the reports. During this time they grew to respect each other as professionals and also developed personal rapport.

One night in the middle of the engagement, Steve and Janie were relaxing in the lounge after a hard day. One thing led to another and the night was spent in Janie's room. They remained lovers for the remainder of the engagement.

Both Steve and Janie found that their affair actually enhanced their productivity on the job. For the duration of their trip they literally lived with the filing and with each other. Although neither had anticipated a long-run affair, they decided to remain lovers upon their return to New York.

Eventually Steve's wife found out about the affair. She reacted with a great deal of anger and filed for divorce. This was particularly hard on Steve's children, to whom he was close. On the other hand, Janie's relationship with her husband had been cool for some time. She was thankful that no children were involved. When Steve moved out of his house, Janie followed him and they got an apartment in Manhattan.

Steve and Janie had the opportunity to work on more engagements together. They found that their relationship actually enhanced their professional productivity, since they would accomplish overtime work and still enjoy each other's company. Many of their professional peers agreed that they worked well together as a team.

Word soon got out in the office about what was going on between Steve and Janie. The people in the office had quite different responses to the affair, yet since it did not upset the working life of the office, most of Steve and Janie's peers were either supportive or neutral about the affair.

Both Steve and Janie were involved in mentoring relationships. The reaction of the mentors was drastically different. Janie talked openly with Ann, her mentor, about the relationship. Ann was basically glad to see that Janie was so happy and used her influence to protect Janie in the office. On the other hand, Steve's mentor Sam was scandalized. He spoke with Steve and counseled him to break off the relationship and return to his family. When Steve refused, Sam terminated the mentoring relationship. Sam even went so far as to speak with Phil, the managing partner of the New York office, and urge that the firm take official action in regard to the relationship.

Questions

1. Comment upon the ethics of office romance. How would deontological and utilitarian ethicists view what happened in this case?
2. How would one who relied upon ethical realism in the profession solve the ethical dilemma involved?
3. Are the personal lives of professional people of legitimate concern to the professional community?
4. Would your response to the case change if Steve and Janie's productivity dramatically decreased because of their affair? Justify your answer based upon ethical principles.
5. Are ethical standards for professional accountants different from those for other businesspersons with respect to office romance? Why or why not?

9-2: CLIENT CONFLICT

Peter is the audit partner in charge of the Cincinnati office of Roberts and Terry, a large international public accounting firm. He has just concluded a business lunch with Chuck, the controller of Cotmore Associates, one of the firm's major clients. At that meeting Peter informed Chuck of a pending change of the partner in charge of the audit at Cotmore.

The relationship between R&T and Cotmore had been an interesting one. Three years ago Peter had taken a big risk in assigning Carol as the partner in charge of the Cotmore audit. The risk involved the fact that Carol was the first female partner of a major firm in the Cincinnati area. Peter had been willing to take the risk because Carol was a highly skilled professional accountant and a shrewd manager who he believed would succeed in the new assignment.

Chuck had been quite dubious about the prospect of having a woman in charge of the audit of Cotmore. Yet at Peter's insistence he went along with the assignment. It was a blockbuster success. Chuck and Carol worked extremely well together and their relationship had become a model of client-auditor rapport around the firm. Moreover, Carol had been able to sell Cotmore several auditing consulting jobs from the management advisory services division of R&T.

At lunch Chuck had expounded to Peter upon how much he respected and appreciated Carol. "I guess I was a classic male chauvinist pig. Carol proved me wrong. She is first class. When she got pregnant I wondered if it would slow her down, but she hasn't skipped a beat. I have grown to trust Carol more than any auditor with whom I have ever worked."

At that point Peter had to inform Chuck that Carol had asked for and been granted a maternity leave. Will, who had recently been promoted to partner, would be in charge of the Cotmore audit for this year. Chuch said that he would miss Carol, but he certainly understood and that he would look forward to working with Will.

Eight months later Peter called Chuck on the phone. The following conversation took place:

Peter: I've got great news for you, Chuck. Carol is returning from maternity leave. She is quite anxious to re-establish her client base. Since you two get along so well, I've decided to put her back on the Cotmore audit.

Chuck: I don't know Peter. We have finally gotten used to Will around here and are pretty pleased with his work. I'm not sure I'm ready for another switch. Besides, what if Carol decides to get pregnant and abandons us again?

Peter: Chuck, I don't think what Carol does with her personal life is really your business.

Chuck: Well, maybe not, but what affects Cotmore Associates is my business. We have already experienced one upheaval because of changes in auditor and we are quite pleased with the way Will has worked out. In fact, I was just talking to him today about the possibility of a new consulting service R&T is offering. But if you can't provide me with some stability, then all bets are off. There will not only be no consulting work, I'll also recommend to the board that we get a new audit firm. Find someone else to juggle your client load with.

Questions

1. What action should Peter take? Defend your position.
2. Using an ethical model, convince Chuck of the rightness or wrongness of his position with respect to Carol.
3. What problems do you foresee for Carol in rebuilding her client base? What actions, if any, should Peter take to assist her? In your response consider the repercussions to the other young partners in the firm.

NOTES

1. P. G. Cottell and C. M. Michael, "Support Relationships and Women in Public Accounting," Unpublished working paper at Miami University, 1990.
2. B. T. Acken, "Upward Bound," *New Accountant*, November 1988, pp. 16–21.
3. American Institute of Certified Public Accountants, *Restatement of the Code of Professional Ethics* (AICPA, 1973).
4. I. Kant, *Grounding for the Metaphysics of Morals*, trans. J. W. Ellington (Indianapolis, Ind.: Hackett, 1981).
5. Acken, "Upward Bound," pp. 16–17.
6. American Institute of Certified Public Accountants, *Upward Mobility of Women: Special Committee Report to the AICPA Board of Directors* (AICPA, 1988).
7. See also J. Skow, "The Myth of Male Housework," *Time*, August 7, 1989, p. 62.
8. R. Lacayo, "A Hard Nose and a Short Skirt," *Time*, November 14, 1988, p. 98.
9. M. McLoughlin, et al., "Men vs. Women," *U.S. News & World Report*, August 8, 1988, pp. 50–57.
10. AICPA, 1988, pp. 4–5.
11. L. A. Mainiero, *Office Romance* (New York: Rawson Associates, 1989).

12. Ibid., p. 45.
13. Ibid., p. 243.
14. For a more detailed discussion of sexual static see P. H. Werhane, "Sexual Static and the Idea of Professional Objectivity," in A. R. Gini and T. Sullivan, eds., *It Comes with the Territory: An Inquiry Concerning Work and the Person* (New York: Random House, 1989).

10

THE PURSUIT OF JUSTICE: SOCIAL RESPONSIBILITY ACCOUNTING

Francis de Sales, controller of the Genesee Cable Company, was not pleased with the way the meeting of the management group had gone. At the meeting, the sales manager Teresa Avila had given a brilliant presentation, at the end of which she had recommended that cable service from the Casual Network be offered as part of their regular package in order to boost cable subscriptions. What disturbed Francis was that Casual's fare was widely regarded as soft pornography, a type of television to which Francis was opposed on moral grounds.

At first, John Cross, the president, had seemed to object. John recalled that when Genesee had been competing for the franchise in this community he had stated at a public hearing that Genesee had no intention of offering pornographic material of any type over the cable service. He wondered aloud whether taking on the Casual station wouldn't be breaking a promise to the community.

Yet Teresa had persisted. She noted that a statement made at a public hearing was not legally binding. She also cited her market research, which showed demand for Casual from many people in the community who were not currently subscribers. What galled Francis most was the fact that Teresa was able to use accounting numbers properly developed in his department to show that by adopting her recommendation Genesee would improve its profits dramatically. At the end of the meeting John seemed to be swayed by the profitability argument, although he did say he wanted to reflect on the recommendation a bit further.

After returning to his office, Francis mused: "Surely there must be more to business than just the bottom line. It seems so irresponsible to break our promise to the community for the sake of making more money. I wonder if accounting, as an information system, might not assign some sort of *value* to the old-fashioned notion of keeping a promise."

INFORMATION ABOUT RESPONSIBILITY

During the 1970s substantial discussion was available in accounting literature about social responsibility accounting. In recent years this topic has been placed on the back burner. Yet, with increasing attention being given to business ethics, we can expect social responsibility accounting to re-emerge as a "hot" topic.

After all, once society decides that ethical behavior is a desired trait to be expected of businesses and business personnel, the logical question will follow: Who is and who is not acting ethically or responsibly? This question creates a demand for *information*, and accounting is one place to which we turn for information about business enterprise. In this chapter we will discuss the difficult yet fascinating role accountants might play in the emerging public concern about business and social responsibility.

ETHICS AND ACCOUNTING REPORTS

K.V. Ramanathan, a leading proponent of social responsibility accounting, defines it as "the process of selecting firm-level social performance variables, measures, and measurement procedures; systematically developing information useful for evaluating the firm's social performance; and communicating such information to concerned social groups, both within and outside the firm."[1] A key accounting role seems apparent here. Accounting, as the language of business, is a primary provider of information. Traditional accounting concerns itself with financial information. In expanding the purview of providing information, we may be going beyond data and interpretation that are clearly financial. Yet ethical process and content may also be "accounted for."

Social responsibility accounting must somehow transform ethical information, which accountants may find "squishy," into financial information, or at least information in financial terms, so that accountants preparing and interpreting the reports are within their professional sphere. The task here is a formidable one. Accountants must work with identified users of information to ascertain what sort of information is required. Then management must decide whether such information should be reported and, if so, in what form. Once these two barriers are surmounted, the accounting profession will be better able to satisfy the need by coming up with the "how" of reporting.

Much debate has occurred about the desirability of even having social responsibility accounting. Its proponents have suggested several models as starting points for developing this kind of accounting. Our intention is to examine the notion of social responsibility from the point of view of ethics.

In Chapter 1 we described the two major ethical theories, utilitarianism and deontologism. Utilitarianism can and has been used to create a good case for accountants not to engage in social responsibility accounting. We will summarize this utilitarian argument in the next section. Following that we will present a deontological case in favor of social responsibility accounting.

UTILITARIAN ARGUMENTS

Opponents of social responsibility accounting argue in an analytical rather than descriptive fashion. That is, they approach the entire issue from the standpoint of cost/benefit analysis. Most accountants are quite comfortable with this type of analysis.

Cost/benefit analysis is a concept that is deeply rooted in utilitarian ethics. In this analysis the utility defined—that is, the good we maximize—is material wealth expressed in terms of dollars. Simply stated, we sum the cost of an action and compare it with the sum of the economic benefits expressed in financial terms. Under a utilitarian criterion we should undertake a project where the economic benefits exceed the costs.

As an example of this kind of utilitarian reasoning, let's return to the Genesee Cable Company. As part of her research concerning the Casual Network, Teresa asked Francis to provide her a differential cost schedule. This kind of managerial report is a common one in accounting. The one that Francis gave to Teresa is shown in Table 10.1.

The differential cost schedule clearly points to the decision to accept Casual Network programming. The operating income with this option exceeds operating income without it by $162,000. Using the terminology of cost/benefit analysis, we can say that the benefits exceed the costs. This is a straightforward case, since both the benefits and the costs may be clearly identified when the utility that we seek to maximize is monetary wealth measured in dollars.

A careful analysis of the social responsibility accounting issue on this utilitarian ground provides disappointing results for its proponents. From the standpoint of the corporation, the costs of placing any new accounting system into place are substantial. Here the

Table 10.1
Genesee Cable Company: Differential Cost Schedule, Casual Network Proposal

	With Casual Network	Without Casual Network	Differential
Cable Subscriptions	$8,150,000	$7,550,000	$600,000
Variable Costs:			
Fees to Networks	$4,700,000	$4,500,000	$200,000
Customer Service	$ 194,000	$ 151,000	$ 43,000
Total Variable Costs	$4,894,000	$4,651,000	$243,000
Contribution Margin	$3,256,000	$2,899,000	$357,000
Fixed Operating Expenses:			
Advertising and Promotion	$1,385,000	$1,320,000	$ 65,000
Cable Maintenance	$ 65,000	$ 65,000	$ 0
Corporate Headquarters	$ 790,000	$ 790,000	$ 0
One Time Fee to Casual	$ 130,000	$ 0	$130,000
Total Fixed Costs	$2,370,000	$2,175,000	$195,000
Operating Income	$ 886,000	$ 724,000	$162,000

company must consider more than the immediate costs of designing and implementing such an accounting system. Also included should be the possible consequences (costs) of publicly reporting the company's actions in the social responsibility arena. An honest reporting of these matters could bring consequences that are not in the best interests of the owners or managers of the corporation. These might come in the form of possible calls for increased government action in the affairs of the company, possible action against the company from special interest groups, or lawsuits from parties who believe they have sustained injury from the company's actions. Moreover, these costs of implementing social responsibility accounting are fairly easy to measure using conventional business forecasting methods. We may thus be fairly certain about the magnitude of the costs.

Against these costs we should weigh the benefits of social responsibility accounting. Here we run into problems, particularly as far as the accountant is concerned. Accounting tends to deal with information that is specific in nature. Within accounting certain types of information are sanctioned as real and true. Accountants therefore focus their attention upon this type of information to the exclusion of other kinds.

The benefits of reporting social responsibility information fall into a category of information that is not currently sanctioned by accounting. Much of the benefit of ethical behavior is not obviously financial in nature. Accountants are therefore understandably uncomfortable with attempts to measure this information, let alone report upon it. The benefits of going through this effort are therefore elusive and difficult to express in financial terms.

By way of example, let's return to the Genesee Cable Company. Certainly utilitarian arguments may be made to reject Teresa's plan to schedule Casual's programming. In the long run the public, in perceiving that Genesee is a company that keeps its promises and is concerned with community values, will be anxious to have increased business contact with Genesee. In accounting terms we might be tempted to call this goodwill. Yet accountants have recognized the problems associated with measuring goodwill for years. Today this task is not even attempted unless the goodwill is demonstrated by a purchase transaction on the open market.

The economically rational manger would be hard pressed not to offer Casual's programming, especially if he attempted to use cost/benefit analysis in arriving at a decision. The possible benefits of a future good name in the community seem somewhat smaller than the prospect of an increase in profit of $162,000 when we take the cost/benefit point of view.

Thus the use of cost/benefit analysis as a criterion for the desirability of social responsibility accounting usually leaves us with heavy, easy-to-measure costs on one hand balanced against vague and seemingly small benefits on the other. Many accounting writers who have looked at the issue of social responsibility accounting from this utilitarian perspective have been quite pessimistic about its future in accounting. Indeed, the practical application of socially responsible actions themselves finds nearly insurmountable hurdles from a cost/benefit point of view. Yet there are underlying weaknesses in attempts to use cost/benefit analysis or any other utilitarian system in a practical way. These have been identified by Alasdair MacIntyre:[2]

1. Utilitarian tests must presuppose the application of some prior non-utilitarian principle that sets limits on the range of activities to be considered.
2. Utilitarian tests must presuppose some method of rank ordering the values of good and evil. This method must be non-utilitarian.
3. Different agents will make different assessments of harms and benefits.

4. The question of what is to count as a consequence of a given action must be answered. Boundaries must be placed upon responsibility for consequences.
5. A time scale must be used in assessing consequences. The question of how far the present should be sacrificed for the future requires a non-utilitarian answer.

These weaknesses of the practical application of utilitarianism readily appear in the use of cost/benefit analysis to assess the usefulness of social responsibility accounting. As we have discussed, the weakness of a non-utilitarian principle is encountered in the fact that accounting has traditionally dealt solely with financial information. The ethical benefits in cost/benefit analysis are often difficult to translate into financial terms. Thus, many accountants are uncomfortable entering into this realm.

Cost/benefit analysis presupposes that material wealth is the sole good to be considered. Thus an arbitrary, non-utilitarian method is assumed at the beginning of the utilitarian reasoning process. Yet reasonable people do not really believe that the accumulation of wealth is the only criterion to look at with respect to good and evil.

The final three weaknesses of practical utilitarianism are particularly evident in examining the benefit side of cost/benefit analysis. Hence the frustration with social responsibility accounting among so many accountants. Different agents translate the benefits into financial terms at different amounts. To many accountants this appears to violate the principle of verifiability. Which consequence of an action is the subject of measurement for the accountant also arises. Finally, the entire matter of comparing the present value of probable future benefits with the costs incurred now is a particularly sticky one in cost/benefit analysis.

We see that the deck seems stacked against not only social responsibility accounting but also socially responsible action when we attempt to apply utilitarian arguments. Yet the economic system in which corporations and their managers operate motivates them to take a utilitarian perspective. Compounding this are forces in the business community that encourage managers to look to short-term rather than long-term results. A change in the underlying way we view the role of the corporation in society can enable us to more realistically assess not only the need for socially responsible action but also the ways accounting can assist managers and outside readers of accounting reports in the tough choices with respect to these actions. This change is to move toward a deontological perspective.

THE DEONTOLOGICAL VIEW

The use of deontologism for the professions in general and for accounting in particular is not new. Lawyers who defend clients' interests irrespective of the general consequences use deontological reasons to justify this behavior. Scientists frequently make inquiry into areas where an answer may lead to bad consequences (atomic power, for example). In medicine the doctrine of informed consent, whereby a patient is not subjected to an experiment without his full knowledge and approval, is well entrenched. Many accountants agree that the Financial Accounting Standards Board should use representative faithfulness (a deontological perspective) over economic consequences (a utilitarian perspective) as a criterion for standard setting.

Moreover, the accounting profession in general and certified public accountants in particular have taken great pains to present their field to society as a profession. It has been asserted in Chapter 2 that well-established professions possess several common characteristics. Among them are that each is governed by ethical principles that emphasize the virtues of self-subordination, honesty, probity, and devotion to the welfare of those served. CPAs have obligations not only to those served but also to third parties. In fact, the obligations to third parties may supersede the obligation to the party about which the CPA issues a report.

DEONTOLOGICAL FRAMEWORK

Deontological ethics can be applied to situations only if an obligation can be satisfied. In Chapter 1 we introduced the ideas of W. D. Ross, a prominent philosopher of the twentieth century. He provided specific criteria to be used as tests for the existence of an obligation and suggested a set of prima facie duties that represent the main moral convictions of the "plain man."[3]

1. Fidelity
2. Reparation
3. Gratitude
4. Justice
5. Beneficence
6. Self-improvement
7. Non-maleficence

We suggest that this list may serve as a starting point for discussion about whether corporations have reporting responsibilities with respect to social responsibility. Two questions must be addressed at the outset. First, do organizations such as corporations have duties that apply to the "plain man?" Second, how shall we know whether a specific duty applies to a particular organization?

Some modern ethicists argue that corporations are moral persons. This is true because people are behind the corporate veil and these people make decisions with moral implications. Society therefore cannot condone as amoral corporate actions that would be considered immoral for the individuals who actually make decisions for the corporation. Portions of the Foreign Corrupt Practices Act that hold corporate officers personally responsible for corporate actions serve as an example of this premise.

P. H. Werhane convincingly takes the issue of corporate social responsibility a step farther in *Persons, Rights, and Corporations*. She argues that corporations have responsibilities apart from the individual responsibilities of persons behind the corporate veil. She demonstrates that corporations argue for legal rights that must have a moral basis if they are justified. An example of this is the enforcement of contracts, which depends upon the moral duty of fidelity. Moreover, "If corporations have moral rights, then they have the obligations connected with such rights, and they can be held accountable, *morally* accountable."[4]

If the prima facie duties apply correctly to individuals, including individuals who manage corporations, then they apply to corporations themselves. We may therefore turn to the second question of how to ascertain whether a specific duty applies to a corporation. S. E. Toulmin has provided a test that may be applied to the prima facie duties:

> In any particular community, certain principles are current—that is to say, attention is paid to certain types of argument as appealing to accepted criteria of "real goodness," "real rightness," "real obligation," etc. From these the members of the community are expected to regulate their lives and judgements. And such a set of principles of "prima facie obligations" of "categorical imperatives" is what we call the "moral code" of the community.[5]

As citizens, readers of financial reports should be concerned about the actions a company is taking or failing to take in the realm of social responsibility. The socially responsible corporation should therefore report upon how it is meeting or failing to meet its duties to the public. Research among investors and other stakeholders indicates that they are in fact interested in corporate activities that fall within the scope of the prima facie duties. We now explain each of these in terms of the business and accounting community.

Fidelity

Fidelity is the first of two duties that rest upon previous acts. Fidelity is simply the keeping of promises. The promises to be kept may be explicit or implicit.

Many explicit promises are already recognized and reported by corporations. Warranties, for example, are accounted for as contingency liabilities with a corresponding expense. Duties stemming from explicit promises may also raise ethical questions that are not so easily recognized in financial terms.

Let us return to the cable television company case with which we began the chapter. Management here is faced with a hard choice between its often-stated duty to maximize return for stockholders and the moral duty to keep the corporation's promise. We have demonstrated how the accounting system through the commonly used differential cost schedule uses utilitarian reasoning to report upon future consequences of managerial action. We have shown that such purely utilitarian reasoning, when used alone, would rarely motivate a manager to choose the socially responsible course of action. Yet Francis, and perhaps John, believe that a duty exists here because of the statements made at the public hearing. The duty that they recognize is fidelity.

From the accountant's viewpoint, can a report be developed to assist the decision-making process from a deontological perspective? Moreover, once the choice is made, can it be reported to interested stakeholders in an accounting context? We assert that in both cases the answer is yes, and we shall return to this example later in the chapter.

Reparation

Duties of reparation rest upon a previous wrongful act of the one who has the duty. Examples of duties of reparation in business are quite common and well publicized. The poison gas leak at the Union Carbide plant in Bhopal, India, and Manville's asbestos-related problems provide recent examples. In both cases the victims of actions taken by the company have received monetary compensation.

A clear reporting problem appears to exist in both the Union Carbide and Manville cases; yet, the wrongful act need not be so dramatic for a duty to arise. Suppose our cable television enterprise decides to proceed with the soft pornography offering. Later Francis learns that a father accused of sexually abusing his four-year-old daughter claims that he was motivated to do so after watching a show on Genesee Cable.

Clearly no legal liability exists here under current law. Yet, ethics are usually considered to be on a higher plane than the law. Therefore a duty with corresponding social responsibility accounting implications may arise when no legal liability is present.

Suppose John, Teresa, and Francis are struck with conscience in this matter and therefore are considering paying for the treatment of the little girl. Their consideration might arise from a sense of duty of reparation. Should they later decide to have Genesee make these payments, a social responsibility accounting implication may have been created.

The management of a particular corporation would have the responsibility of deciding the corporation's ethical standards with respect to reparation. The accountant's role would be to report upon the financial implications of meeting those standards. Such reporting might be internal or external. A corporate decision not to accept a reparation duty could also be a reportable event under social responsibility accounting.

Gratitude

Duties of gratitude arise from services done by others for the one who has the duty of gratitude. At first the notion of corporate gratitude may seem questionable, yet official communication from corporations often express gratitude. Annual reports of companies frequently express corporate appreciation for a job well done by employees. Gratitude can be more specific. When Frank Cary retired as the chairman of the board of International Business Machines, the new chairman stated that the company was "indebted" to him "for the wisdom and skill with which he led the company."[6]

The duty of gratitude is not only owed employees. A company might have reason to be grateful to a community, to suppliers, to customers, or to others who interact with it. The duty arises because of the previous actions of the other entities.

A question of interest with respect to social responsibility accounting is whether the gratitude expressed by corporations has an associated duty, and whether there is a future cost associated with the duty. If a corporation appreciates efforts by its loyal employees, has a duty been created for the corporation to those employees when economic times are not so good? Does indebtedness of IBM imply that a duty exists? Moreover, if the answers to these questions are yes, what are the costs of fulfilling these duties or not fulfilling them?

On the other hand, a company need not express gratitude for the duty to exist. From the standpoint of ethics an unrecognized duty might exist. Social responsibility accounting may be one vehicle that could assist managers and others in recognizing this duty.

Justice

Duties of justice rest on the fact or possibility of a distribution of pleasure or happiness (or the means thereto) that is not in accordance with the merit of the persons concerned. A duty may arise in such cases to upset or prevent such a distribution. Corporations are frequently confronted with duties that arise from justice. Such duties would create reporting implications under social responsibility accounting.

Suppose that a large corporation is headquartered in a maturing city that contains a ghetto. The youth of the ghetto are unable to attain employment at the corporation because, due to circumstances beyond their control, they are unqualified. In such circumstances enlightened management may believe that it is their duty, and by connection the corporation's, to overturn this state of affairs by providing job training programs. Such a sense of duty would arise from a concern for justice.

Notice that in this case the sense of duty did not arise from any previous action or promise of the corporation or its management. Duties of justice arise simply because an observed situation is wrong per se. If the corporation recognizes such a duty, a cost may ensue in the future should the corporation create a training program, for example.

Of interest here is that the corporation does not internalize an externality that it created, an often heard reason for socially responsible action, nor does the corporation take action because it believes that the training program will benefit it in the long run (a utilitarian argument). Rather the action is undertaken due to a sense of duty.

The duty arises from a concept of justice, perhaps best stated by John Rawls. "Justice is the virtue of practices where there are assumed to be competing interests and conflicting claims and where it is supposed that persons will press their rights on each other. That persons are mutually self-interested in certain situations and for certain purposes is what gives rise to the questioning of justice in practices couching those circumstances."[7] Rawls argues that every person may be supposed to have a concept of justice. This proposition is true because each person is involved in some relationships with others. In the context of these relationships each person forms a concept of justice for herself as well as for others. Corporate persons would be among those under this societal umbrella.

Beneficence

Like duties of justice, duties of beneficence do not arise because of any culpability on the part of the corporation. Duties of beneficence rest upon the mere fact that there are other beings in the world whose condition can be made better. If the corporation recognizes these beings and is able to improve their condition, then a duty of beneficence arises.

The fact that duties of beneficence are recognized by managers of corporations is demonstrated by the fact that they cause the corporations to make charitable contributions. One is hard pressed to swallow utilitarian reasoning that such contributions may in the long run improve profitability by the creation of goodwill. In fact, the best arguments against such action are utilitarian in nature. Milton Friedman represents perhaps the best-known proponent of this utilitarian point of view.

The Philip Morris Company is well known in some circles as a supporter of the arts. Yet this company does not have a great deal of goodwill in general. Contributions to the ballet are not made in the hope of generating cigarette sales. They are made because people who work for this company believe that society will benefit from having the arts more widely available to the public. In other words, the donations are made because of a sense of duty, the duty of beneficence.

Duties of beneficence on the part of corporations are recognized in the tax laws, in that amounts spent for charity are deductible for tax purposes. They provide an interesting twist in that the duty recognized by the corporation is externalized. Persons who may not recognize the duty become partners in fulfilling the duty in the sense that the government receives less revenue from the corporate source.

Self-Improvement

Duties of self-improvement are the most difficult of Ross's duties of individuals to translate to a corporation. Duties of self-improvement rest on the fact that one can improve her own condition with respect to virtue or intelligence. Interestingly, Ross includes pleasure in the improvement of another's condition but omits it in the improvement of one's own condition.

The difficulty with respect to duties of self-improvement lies in defining the corporation when viewing it as something where virtue or knowledge warrant improvement. However, if we accept the notion a priori that a corporation improves itself when it improves its management, duties of self-improvement may be found. An example is the practice of companies paying the cost of sending managers to universities to improve their education. Utilitarians would undoubtedly argue that such action is taken to improve profits through lower costs generated from the better management the corporation expects to receive from better-educated managers. Corporations would undeniably justify this practice on such utilitarian grounds.

However, the imagination must truly be stretched to translate an individual manager's education to the bottom line. A more plausible explanation for such things as classes in human relations might be found in the desire to fulfill a duty for self-improvement. If this is true, does the public bear costs when a corporation does not recognize such a duty? For example, one could argue that by failure to improve managers' knowledge of business ethics, a corporation has caused the public to incur greater risk of unethical conduct by the corporation.

The duty of self-improvement becomes one we may more easily associate with business enterprise if we expand upon Ross's definition a bit. A commonly held and frequently cited belief is that business corporations have the duty to make profits. We may easily accept this notion by stating that the company has the duty to improve itself by improving its financial position. As we do this we agree with Ross that the duty of self-improvement should be subordinated to the other duties.

Non-Maleficence

This is the only duty that is stated in a negative way. Non-maleficence is the duty not to injure others. Duties of non-maleficence are clearly the most compelling; violations of these duties create debate about corporate irresponsibility.

Pollution can serve as an example of how deontological ethics is superior to utilitarian ethics in solving dilemmas. A utilitarian argument for pollution may be made on the basis that those who pollute will generate more profit than those who incur costs to avoid pollution. Yet, reasonable men and women view pollution as undesirable.

The utilitarian solution to this dilemma is to argue that the externalities created by the pollution involve more bad than the good created by the profits. The logical conclusion to the utilitarian view is that the responsible corporation should pollute just up to the point where the pollution will not exceed the good generated by the profit and no further. These arguments do not represent the attitudes of plain-thinking people. Indeed, most reasonable people could agree that pollution of the air and water is a prima facie wrong. It is wrong because it is injurious to others irrespective of utility. Because pollution is wrong, members of society, including corporate members, have a duty not to engage in the practice. This is the duty of non-maleficence.

The implications for social responsibility accounting are perhaps most clear under duties of non-maleficence. In the pollution example, those companies that internalize the cost of pollution by purchasing anti-pollution equipment have done their duty and would so report. Those who do not incur these costs will make higher profits, but should be required to report as a social cost the damage the pollution has done or will do.

The duty of non-maleficence could also apply in the Genesee Cable case. As part of his consideration of Teresa's proposal, John might recall an article that asserts that men who watch pornographic material on television develop an attitude toward women that views them as objects to be exploited rather than persons to be respected. If John believes this article, he may decide against accepting Teresa's proposal on the grounds that he does not desire Genesee to be a party to fostering such attitudes in the community. In this case he would be acting out of the duty of non-maleficence.

TOWARD SOCIAL RESPONSIBILITY ACCOUNTING

M. R. Mathews has suggested an excellent classification system through which accounting researchers may look at social accounting. We shall use this framework to suggest how deontological ethics may be incorporated into social accounting. Under the system, social accounting is divided into two parts, defined by Mathews as social responsibility accounting (SRA) and total impact accounting (TIA) respectively.

> [SRA is] voluntary disclosure of information both qualitative and quantitative, made by organizations to inform or influence a range of audiences. The quantitative disclosures may be in financial or non-financial terms.
>
> The term Total Impact Accounting (TIA) refers to attempts at measuring, in monetary terms, the total cost of running an organization in its existing form. The total cost of running an organization may be divided between private and public costs.[8]

Social Responsibility Accounting

SRA differs from TIA in that the former is shorter range in nature and does not precisely measure in financial terms for the most part. TIA measures precisely and incorporates social responsibility into the overall accounting system. TIA may be regarded as a more sophisticated or mature form of accounting than SRA. In fact, social costs of the organization would evolve from a SRA system into a TIA system.

The identification of corporate duties would thus be a first step and would fall under SRA. This step would take place at a level akin to the strategic planning function of the organization. A second step, also a part of SRA, would be to identify those actions, or lack thereof, that would have an impact upon or relate to the organization's duties. The final SRA step would be to decide upon an appropriate internal or external reporting medium to inform interested readers about how the organization was fulfilling its self-defined duties.

Total Impact Accounting

The challenge from an accounting standpoint is moving from SRA to TIA. Private costs, as envisioned by TIA, are those costs with which the accounting system of most organizations already deals effectively. The familiar production costs of material, labor, and overhead as well as the periodic expenses of the organization readily come to mind.

Public costs, then, are those that for the most part are borne by society. These public costs are more commonly called externalities. Note that externalities may result in either cost or gain to society. So the plant that pollutes the air in a particular community (a public cost) may also benefit that community through capital formation and the payment of wages (a public gain).

Total impact accounting provides the broad classification into which the deontological basis suggested here will fit. The classifications system could take the form of accounts set up for each of the duties that a company has chosen as applicable to it. So if all the Ross duties were deemed appropriate, the company would set into place seven social responsibility accounts, one for each identified duty. Since doing one's duty has an associated impact upon profit, an account would also be created to summarize those effects over periods of time. We will call this latter account social capital.

A great deal of research needs to be done to perfect TIA. However, we can envision a new statement of social responsibility where public costs and public gains are reported. Public cost would be debited when the corporation, having identified its duty, is either unwilling or unable to fulfill it. Public gain would be credited when the corporation takes necessary steps to do its duty, thereby lowering its profits. The yearly balance of the public costs and gains could be held in an account, social capital, which would be similar to retained earnings.

A "Resolution" of the Genesee Cable Case

Let us return to the cable television hypothetical with which we started the chapter. In this case the management of the company is faced with the hard choice of offering sexually explicit material after promising not to do so. Offering this programming would increase profits. Forgoing the offering fulfills the duties of fidelity and non-maleficence. It might also preclude the duty of reparation in the future.

Under total impact accounting, offering the programming would create a public cost and be so reported. Conversely, forgoing the offering would be reported as a public gain. The amount to be reported would be the amount by which profits increased or were expected to increase as a result of offering the sexually explicit material. Referring back to the differential cost schedule, we would use $162,000 as the amount to be debited to public cost or credited to public gain. The differential cost schedule serves as an objective document from which the amounts can be verified.

A POSITIVE APPROACH

Much of the current negative reaction to social accounting is due to the utilitarian criticism that corporations have created bad consequences by their past actions. Therefore, they should engage in a sort of public repentance, admit their evil ways, and formally report upon this through accounting. Businesspersons, understandably, do not view such suggestions with much favor.

A deontological perspective takes a more positive and more acceptable point of view. Business is asked not to be morally good but to take right actions, thus relieving businesspersons of the concern that their actions will be second-guessed from a moral point of view due to consequences. An aspect of this viewpoint is that the decision not to act is in itself an action. If one can alter circumstances but decides not to do so, then one must take responsibility for the omission just as one must take responsibility for an overt act.

Management Responsibility

The task of formulating and stating the responsibilities deemed appropriate for a particular company rests with the management of the company. That management should believe a company has responsibilities is suggested by social contract theory. Under this theory corporations function within society and require its sanction for their continued existence. A so-called "social contract" is thereby created, which implies that corporations owe society something in return. By formulating responsibilities and discharging them, corporations may be able to fulfill their part of the social contract.

That managers do in fact believe they have responsibility toward society has been suggested by several writers. For the most part, managers do not ponder whether or not they should do the right thing. Rather, they seek to know what the right action is.

The penalty for not properly defining the right action is severe. K. Davis has stated that there is an Iron Law of Responsibility: "In the long run, those who do not use power in the manner which society considers responsible will tend to lose it."[9] Businesses that do not establish a track record of responsible decisions are threatened with the prospect of sharing their decision-making discretion with government and with representatives of special interest groups.

The formulation of responsibilities can make the task of properly defining right action an easier one throughout the organization. Moreover, the publication of corporate responsibilities in the form of duties is a proper step in demonstrating responsible action. Taking right action based on these duties can assist the organization in fulfilling it obligation to society and avoiding the penalty of the Iron Law of Responsibility.

The Role of Accounting

The accountant is a key professional involved in assisting management with the task of setting responsibilities and with monitoring progress toward meeting such responsibilities. This may be accomplished by classifying each responsibility perceived by management as a corporate duty under the deontological framework of total impact accounting. Accountants would be responsible for reporting on "how well we are doing," not only in purely profit and loss terms but also in terms of "fulfilling our duty to society."

Further research into total impact accounting may reveal appropriate ways to report upon fulfilling corporate duties. In many cases this would be an internal reporting issue only, so that management can monitor progress toward their responsibility objective and the cost of fulfilling their duties. In other cases management may wish to report to financial statement readers what duties they believe the company has and what private costs have been incurred to reach the public gains.

With respect to external reporting, several writers have noted that managers would naturally have a bias toward reporting the socially responsible actions that they have taken. Correspondingly, they would be reluctant to report upon the organization's ethical failures. Accountants should view this as an opportunity for an increase in their role through the auditing function. The so-called social auditor can monitor total impact accounting much the same as the financial auditor monitors financial statements. The increase in professional responsibility would be both internal and public.

AN EXPANSION OF HORIZON

The argument has been made that adequate measurement tools do not exist to make social accounting feasible. This argument should not be construed as a reason to abandon social accounting but rather as a call for additional research into the area. The body of accounting knowledge is not static but exceedingly dynamic. A statement made by R. T. De George concerning business ethics applies equally well to ethics in accounting:

> Business ethics does not consist simply in applying ethical theory or moral norms to cases in business—although it includes this sort of activity. To stop here is to imply that, although these are new cases, there is nothing new to learn in the field, there is no research required or appropriate, and there is nothing new to be discovered. . . . If there is a field of business ethics, and if it does not consist simply in applying moral norms or ethical theory to cases in business, it will develop and grow only if there is research to be done and that research is done. The results of such research, as the results of any research, can be taught to students.[10]

Accounting should be developed to provide information to management on the financial implications of acting or failing to act upon ethical issues. If this is accomplished, research into social responsibility accounting can go hand in hand with research in business ethics. A deontological framework provides a starting place for the conduct of such research. By accepting a positive, deontological approach to modern social and ethical issues, accountants will be better able to serve society and thus enhance their claim to ethical professionalism. The task is not an easy one, but the end will not be accomplished unless work is begun.

CASE STUDIES

10-1: RESPONSIBILITY FOR REPORTING

Chris is an internal auditor with the Electro-Solvent Corporation. She had recently returned from a routine inventory visit to one of the company's sites in West Virginia. While relaxing in a motel lounge, she overheard a conversation that startled her and aroused her professional curiosity.

Some men from the state environmental protection agency were discussing their activities of the day and disclosed that they involved Electro-Solvent. "It looks as if we have discovered yet another undisclosed toxic waste site here. That's typical for Electro-Solvent. They have over a dozen questionable sites in the state that we know about. By the time we get through with them they will be out over a half-billion bucks in cleanup costs."

When Chris got home she consulted some of the managers about this and discovered that indeed there were several sites that would require cleanup and that the potential was in the hundreds of millions of dollars, more than enough to bankrupt Electro-Solvent. When Chris asked the controller about reporting this potential liability, she gave her several reasons why the amount was not disclosed on the 10-K or the annual report.

1. The company already made footnote disclosure about environmental concerns. Chris noted this disclosure stated that the company did not believe the amounts to be material.
2. Since the amount of potential liability was unknown and in the future, the company did not want to unduly worry stakeholders.
3. The company intended to sue its insurance company for the amounts in question. Company attorneys believed that they had a reasonable chance to prevail.
4. The independent auditors were permitting the disclosure as currently stated.

Questions

1. What social responsibility accounting issues can you identify in the case?

2. Suggest ways that the potential liability might be booked.
3. What, if any, actions are suggested for Chris should management decide not to disclose this matter any further?

10-2: RESPONSIBILITY TO STAKEHOLDERS

Bob Waggener came to work in an extremely expansive mood. As sales manager of the Patch Furniture Company he found himself in an enviable position. The company had orders for its furniture that far exceeded its capacity. This was in spite of the fact that Patch had recently announced a substantial price increase. All of this was occurring just a few months after most of Patch's competitors had closed their factories and declared insolvency.

Patch's very survival at this time was largely due to the efforts of Bob. The company had just come through a period of severe economic hardship for the furniture industry. During this period Bob had cultivated personal relationships with many small, rural furniture stores. While Patch's competitors were languishing due to a lack of orders from large department stores and retail chains, Patch was barely able to sustain itself with the orders of these small stores. Many of these stores were intensely loyal to Bob and to Patch, even to the point of resisting intense price competition from Patch's desperate competitors.

Bob was looking forward to the meeting this morning that the company president, Sally Duke, had called. When he arrived at the meeting, he found the controller, Barbara West, was also there.

Sally: Bob, I want to congratulate you again for the tremendous job you have done for us over the years. It is obvious that we are now in a position to become extremely profitable now that we have survived that recession.

Barbara: I agree with Sally, Bob, but I now believe the time has come to look forward. Reports coming out of my shop indicate that the time has come to make a change in our marketing strategy.

Bob: How so?

Barbara: We currently have many orders from some large, regional department stores and one national retail chain. Differential cost studies that I have conducted indicate that the most profitable course of action that we can take, given our current capacity, is to accept these large orders and not the orders from the small stores to which you are inclined to sell.

Sally: Bob, I have studied Barbara's reports and believe she is right. We have the responsibility to our stockholders to maximize Patch's profits.

Bob: Sally, if we deny our regular customers their orders they will be forced out of business. These people were the ones who kept us going during bad times. Surely that counts for something. I know these people and don't want to be part of any action that causes them to suffer.

Questions

1. From a deontological perspective, identify duties suggested by this case. Do any of these duties conflict?
2. Design a means by which a social responsibility accounting system could report the action of accepting orders from small customers and accepting orders from the larger customers.
3. Without using profit maximization as a criterion, suggest a utilitarian solution to this dilemma. Can an accounting system measure the utility that you have chosen?

NOTES

1. K. V. Ramanathan, "Toward a Theory of Corporate Social Accounting," *Accounting Review*, July 1976, p. 518.
2. A. MacIntyre, "Utilitarianism and Cost/Benefit Analysis: An Essay on the Relevance of Moral Philosophy to Bureaucratic Theory," in K. Sayre, ed., *Values in the Electric Power Industry* (Notre Dame, Ind.: Philosophic Institute of the University of Notre Dame, 1977).
3. W. D. Ross, *The Right and the Good* (Oxford, Eng.: Claredon Press, 1930).
4. P. H. Werhane, *Persons, Rights, and Corporations* (Englewood Cliffs, N.J.: Prentice-Hall, 1985), p. 60.
5. S. E. Toulmin, *An Examination of the Place of Reason in Ethics* (Cambridge, Eng.: Cambridge University Press, 1950), p. 140.
6. International Business Machines, *Annual Report*, 1983.
7. J. Rawls, "Justice as Fairness," *Philosophical Review*, 1958, p. 175.
8. M. R. Mathews, "A Suggested Classification for Social Accounting Research," *Journal of Accounting and Public Policy*, Fall 1984, p. 204.
9. K. Davis, "Five Propositions for Social Responsibility," *Business Horizons*, June 1975, p. 20.
10. R. T. De George, "Exploitation and Just Wage," *Social Responsibility: Business, Journalism, Law, Medicine*, 1984, p. 5.

SELECTED BIBLIOGRAPHY

Acken, B. T. "Upward Bound," *New Accountant*, November 1988, pp. 16–21.

Ackerman, B. *Social Justice in the Liberal State*. New Haven: Yale University Press, 1980.

American Institute of Certified Public Accountants. *Restatement of the Code of Professional Ethics*. AICPA, 1973.

______. *Restructuring Professional Standards to Achieve Professional Excellence in a Changing Environment*. AICPA, 1986.

______. *Code of Professional Conduct*, as amended January 12, 1988.

______. *Upward Mobility of Women: Special Committee Report to The AICPA Board of Directors*. AICPA, 1988.

Arrow, K. J. "Social Responsibility and Economic Efficiency," *Public Policy*, Summer 1973, pp. 303–17.

Arthur Andersen & Co. *Answers to Important Questions about Scope of Practice and Auditor Independence*. Arthur Andersen & Co. Societe Cooperative, 1987.

Bartels, Robert. "A Model for Ethics in Marketing." *Journal of Marketing* 31 (1967), pp. 20–26 as cited in Don W. Finn, Lawrence B. Chonko, and Shelby D. Hunt, "Ethical Problems in Public Accounting," *Journal of Business Ethics* 7 (1988), p. 606.

Beach, J. E. "Code of Ethics: The Professional Catch 22," *Journal of Accounting and Public Policy*, Winter 1984, pp. 311–23.

Beauchamp, T. L., and N. E. Bowie. *Ethical Theory and Business*. Englewood Cliffs, N.J.: Prentice-Hall, 1979.

Benston, G. J. "Accounting and Corporate Accountability," *Accounting Organization and Society*, May 1982, pp. 87–105.

______. "Rejoinder to Accounting and Corporate Accountability: An Extended Comment," *Accounting Organization and Society*, June 1984, pp. 417–19.

______. "The Market for Public Accounting Services: Demand, Supply and Regulation," *Journal of Accounting and Public Policy*, Spring 1985, pp. 33–79.

Berg, E. N. "The Big Eight: Still a Male Bastion," *New York Times*, July 22, 1988, pp. 1, 7.

Berstein, R. J. "Nietzche or Aristotle? Reflections on Alasdair MacIntyre's *After Virtue*," *Soundings*, Spring 1984, pp. 6–29.

Berton, L. "Investors Call CPA into Account," *Wall Street Journal*, January 28, 1985, p. 26.

Bigsay, L. "NAA Establishes Ethics Code," *Management Accounting*, August 1983, p. 26.

Bishop, A. C. "Development of a Professional Code of Ethics," *Journal of Accountancy*, May 1987, pp. 97–100.

Blake, D. H., W. C. Frederick, and M. S. Myers. "Measurement Problems in the Social Audit." In *Ethical Theory and Business*. T. L. Beauchamp and N. E. Bowie, eds. Englewood Cliffs, N.J.: Prentice-Hall, 1979, pp. 246–52.

Blau, P. M. *Exchange and Power in Social Life*. New York: Wiley, 1964.

Blumberg, P. I. "Corporate Responsibility and Employees' Duty of Loyalty and Obedience," *Oklahoma Law Review*, August 1971, pp. 271–318.

Bok, S. *Lying: Moral Choice in Public and Private Life*. New York: Random House, 1978.

Brannigan, M. "Auditor's Downfall Shows a Man Caught in a Trap of His Own Making," *Wall Street Journal*, March 4, 1987, p. 33.

Broad, C. D. *Five Types of Ethical Theory*. London: Routledge and Kegan Paul, 1956.

Buckley, J. W. "In Search of Identity." In *Ethics in the Accounting Profession*. S. E. Loeb, ed. New York: Wiley, 1978, pp. 37–50.

Burke, R. J. "Mentors in Organizations," *Group and Organizational Studies*, 1984, pp. 353–72.

Burton, J. C. "A Critical Look at Professionalism and Scope of Services," *Journal of Accountancy*, April 1980, pp. 48–56.

Carey, J. L. "The Realities of Professional Ethics," *Accounting Review*, April 1947, pp. 119–23.

Carey, J. L. and W. O. Doherty. *Ethical Standards of the Accounting Profession*. AICPA, 1966.

"The Case of the Singing CPA," *Newsweek*, July 17, 1989, p. 41.

Chua, W. F. "Radical Developments in Accounting Thought," *Accounting Review*, October 1986, pp. 601–32.

Cook, M. F. "Is the Mentor Relationship Principally a Male Experience?" *Personnel Administrator*, November 1978, pp. 82–86.

Cottell, P. G. "Ethical Grounding Among Managerial Accountants," *Akron Business and Economic Review*, Summer 1987, pp. 31–39.

Davis, K. "Five Propositions for Social Responsibility," *Business Horizons*, June 1975, pp. 19–24.

Davis, M. "Professionalism Means Putting Your Profession First," *Georgetown Journal of Legal Ethics*, Summer 1988, pp. 341, 346.

De George, R. T. "Exploitation and Just Wage," *Social Responsibility: Business, Journalism, Law, Medicine*, 1984, pp. 5–23.

Dierkes, M., and A. B. Antal. "The Usefulness and Use of Social Reporting Information," *Accounting Organization and Society*, January 1985, pp. 29–34.

Dirsmith, M. W., and M. A. Covaleski. "Informal Communications, Nonformal Communications, and Mentoring in Public Accounting Firms," *Accounting Organization and Society*, May 1985, pp. 149–169.

Donagan, A. *The Theory of Morality*. Chicago: University of Chicago Press, 1977.

Durkheim, E. "Professional Ethics and Civic Morals." In *Ethics in the Accounting Profession*. S. E. Loeb, ed. New York: Wiley, 1978, pp. 38–48.

Foot, P. *Virtues and Vices and Other Essays in Philosophy*. Berkeley: University of California Press, 1979.

Frankena, W. *Ethics*. Englewood Cliffs, N.J.: Prentice-Hall, 1963.

French, P. A. "Corporate Moral Agency." In *Ethical Theory and Business*. T. L. Beauchamp and N. E. Bowie, eds. Englewood Cliffs, N.J.: Prentice-Hall, 1979, pp. 175–86.

Friedman, M. "The Social Responsibility of Business Is to Increase Its Profits," *New York Times Magazine*, September 13, 1970, pp. 122–26.

Gewirth, A. *Reason and Morality*. Chicago: University of Chicago Press, 1978.

Gilligan, Carol S. *In a Different Voice: Psychological Theory and Women's Development*. Cambridge, Mass.: Harvard University Press, 1982.

Goldman, A., and B. Barlev. "The Auditor-Firm Conflict of Interests: Its Implications for Independence," *Accounting Review*, October 1974, pp. 707–18.

Goode, W. J. "Community within a Community: The Professions," *American Sociological Review*, 1957, pp. 194–200.

Goodpaster, K. E. "An Agenda for Applied Ethics," *Social Responsibility: Business, Journalism, Law, Medicine*, 1985, pp. 5–13.

Gordon, F. E., and M. H. Strober. *Bringing Women into Management*. New York: McGraw-Hill, 1975.

Greenwood, E. "Attributes of a Profession," *Social Work*, July 1957, pp. 45–59.

Gustafson, J. M. *Ethics from a Theocentric Perspective*. Chicago: University of Chicago Press, 1984.

Hall, W. D. *Accounting and Auditing: Thoughts on Forty Years in Practice and Education*. Chicago: Arthur Andersen & Co., 1987.

Hampshire, S. *Two Theories of Morality*. Oxford, Eng.: Oxford University Press, 1977.

Henning, M., and A. Jardim. *The Managerial Women*. New York: Anchor Press/Doubleday, 1977.

Hoffman, W. M. "The Cost of a Corporate Conscience," *Business and Society Review*, Spring 1989, pp. 46–47.

Homes, R. L. "The Concept of Corporate Responsibility." In *Ethical Theory and Business*. T. L. Beauchamp and N. E. Bowie, eds. Englewood Cliffs, N.J.: Prentice-Hall, 1979.

Hooks, K. L., and S. J. Cheramy. "Coping with Women's Expanding Role in Public Accounting," *Journal of Accountancy*, February 1989, pp. 66–70.

Hoskin, K. W., and R. H. Macve. "Accounting and the Examination: A Genealogy of Disciplinary Power," *Accounting Organization and Society*, April 1986, pp. 105–36.

Hunt, D. M., and C. M. Michael. "Mentorship: A Career Training and Development Tool," *Academy of Management Review*, July 1983, pp. 475–85.

Hymowitz, C. "Stepping Off the Fast Track," *Wall Street Journal*, June 13, 1989, p. B1.

International Business Machines. *Annual Report*, 1983.

Kant, I. *Grounding for the Metaphysics of Morals*. J. W. Ellington, trans. Indianapolis, Ind.: Hackett, 1981.

Kanter, R. M. *Men and Women of the Corporation*. New York: Basic Books, 1977.

Kipnis, K. *Legal Ethics*. Englewood Cliffs, N.J.: Prentice-Hall, 1986.

Kram, K. E. "Phases of the Mentor Relationship," *Academy of Management Journal*, December 1983, pp. 608–25.

Krauthammer, C. "Our Loss of Moral Perspective," *Cincinnati Enquirer*, January 18, 1989, p. A-10.

______. "An Unending Quest for Self-Love," *Cincinnati Enquirer*, May 7, 1989, p. E-3.

Lacayo, R. "A Hard Nose and a Short Skirt," *Time*, November 14, 1988, p. 98.

Larson, M. S. *The Rise of Professionalism*. Berkeley: University of California Press, 1977.

Lavin, D. "Perceptions of the Independence of the Auditor," *Accounting Review*, January 1976, pp. 41–50.

Levinson, D. J., et al. *The Seasons of a Man's Life*. New York: Knopf, 1978.

Levitt, T. "The Progress of Social Responsibility," *Harvard Business Review*, September/October 1958, pp. 41–50.

Lewis, C. S. *God in the Dock*. Grand Rapids, Mich.: William B. Eerdmans, 1978.

Linowes, D. F. *The Corporate Conscience*. New York: Hawthorne, 1974.

Loeb, S. E. *Ethics in the Accounting Profession*. New York: Wiley, 1978.

______. "Codes of Ethics and Self Regulation for Non-public Accountants: A Public Policy Perspective," *Journal of Accounting and Public Policy*, Spring 1984, pp. 1–8.

Loft, A. "Toward a Critical Understanding of Accounting: The Case of Cost Accounting in the U.K.," *Accounting Organization and Society*, April 1986, pp. 105–46.

Lovibond, S. *Realism and Imagination in Ethics*. Minneapolis: University of Minnesota Press, 1983.

Lowe, H. J. "Ethics in Our 100-Year History," *Journal of Accountancy*, May 1987, pp. 78–87.

MacIntyre, A. C. *A Short History of Ethics*. New York: Macmillan, 1966.

______. "Utilitarianism and Cost/Benefit Analysis: An Essay on the Relevance of Moral Philosophy to Bureaucratic Theory." In *Values in the Electric Power Industry*. K. Sayre, ed. Notre Dame, Ind.: Philosophic Institute of the University of Notre Dame, 1977, pp. 217–37.

______. *After Virtue*, 2nd ed. Notre Dame, Ind.: University of Notre Dame Press, 1984.

______. "Bernstein's Distorting Mirrors: A Rejoinder," *Soundings*, Spring 1984, pp. 30–41.

McLoughlin, M. et al. "Men vs. Women," *U.S. News & World Report*, August 8, 1988, pp. 50–57.

Mainiero, L. A. *Office Romance: Love, Power, and Sex in the Workplace*. New York: Rawson Associates, 1989.

Malkiel, B. G., and R. E. Quandt. "Moral Issues in Investment Policy," *Harvard Business Review*, March/April 1971, pp. 37–47.
Mathews, M. R. "A Suggested Classification for Social Accounting Research," *Journal of Accounting and Public Policy*, Fall 1984, pp. 199–221.
May, C. D. "Prosaic Life of Suspect in '71 New Jersey Murders," *New York Times*, June 9, 1989, pp. B1, B4.
Meyer, J. W., and B. Rowan. "Institutional Organizations: Formal Structure as Myth and Ceremony," *American Journal of Sociology*, September 1977, pp. 340–63.
Merz, C. M., and D. F. Hunt. *Toward a Code of Ethics for Management Accountants*. New York: National Association of Accountants, 1981.
Michael, C. M. "Support Relationships in the Career Development of Home Economists in the Home Equipment and Related Product Industries," *Home Economics Research Journal*, March 1988, pp. 163–72.
Michael, C. M., and D. M. Hunt. "Women and Organizations: A Study of Mentorship." In *Preparing Professional Women for the Future: Resources for Teachers and Trainers*. V. J. Ramsey, ed. Ann Arbor, Mich.: University of Michigan Press, 1985, pp. 177–90.
Missirian, A. K. "The Process of Mentoring in the Career Development of Female Managers." Unpublished Doctoral Dissertation, University of Massachusetts, 1980.
Morgan, R. G., H. Soroosh, and C. J. Woelfel. "Are Ethics Dangerous to Your Job?" *Management Accounting*, February 1985, pp. 24–32.
Munson, R. *Intervention and Reflection*. Belmont, Calif.: Wadsworth, 1983.
"NAA Publishes First Code of Ethics for Management Accountants," *Management Accounting*, September 1983, pp. 68–70.
Nash, N. C. "Bank Board Releases Memo on Danger in Examiner Shift," *New York Times*, July 10, 1989, pp. 1, 24.
National Association of Accountants. *Standards of Ethical Conduct for Management Accountants, Statement on Management Accounting* Number 1C. NAA, 1983.
Nozick, R. *Anarchy, State and Utopia*. New York: Basic Books, 1973.
Orth, C. D., and F. Jacobs. "Women in Management: Pattern for Change," *Harvard Business Review*, July/August 1971, pp. 139–47.
Palmer, P. J. *To Know As We Are Known*. New York: Harper and Row, 1983.
Parent, D. E., C. DeAngelis, and N. R. Myers. "Parity for Women CPA's." *Journal of Accountancy*, February 1989, pp. 72–76.
Parfit, D. *Reasons and Persons*. Oxford, Eng.: Oxford University Press, 1984.
Pearson, M. A. "Enhancing Perceptions of Auditor Independence," *Journal of Business Ethics*, February 1985, pp. 53–56.
______. "Auditor Independence Deficiencies and Alleged Audit Failures," *Journal of Business Ethics*, May 1987, pp. 281–87.
Powers, C. W. *People/Profits: The Ethics of Investment*. Washington, D.C.: Council on Religion and International Affairs, 1972.
Rankin, K. "Minority Coalition Attacks Big Mergers," *Accounting Today*, August 20, 1989, pp. 1, 17.
Ramanathan, K. V. "Toward a Theory of Corporate Social Accounting," *Accounting Review*, July 1976, pp. 516–27.

Ransic, C. D. "The Supreme Court and Affirmative Action: An Evolving Standard or Compounded Confusion?" *Employee Relations Law Journal*, Autumn 1988, pp. 175–90.

Rawls, J. "Justice as Fairness," *Philosophical Review*, 1958, pp. 164–94.

———. *A Theory of Justice*. Cambridge, Mass.: Harvard University Press, 1971.

Reich, M. H. "Executive Views from Both Sides of Mentoring," *Personnel*, March 1985, pp. 42–46.

Roche, G. E. "Much Ado about Mentors," *Harvard Business Review*, January/February 1979, pp. 14–28.

Ross, W. D. *The Right and the Good*. Oxford, Eng.: Claredon Press, 1930.

Roy, R. H. and J. H. MacNeill. *Horizons for a Profession*. AICPA, 1967.

Ruland, R. G. "Duty, Obligation, and Responsibility in Accounting Policy Making," *Journal of Accounting and Public Policy*, Fall 1984, pp. 223–37.

Salvadori, M. G. "The Code of Ethics of the American Society of Civil Engineers," *Engineering Issues*, April 1975, pp. 215–19.

Sartorius, R. E. *Individual Conduct and Social Norms: A Utilitarian Account of Social Union and Rule of Law*. Evanston, Ill.: Dickerson Publishing, 1975.

Schaeffer, F. A. *How Should We Then Live?* Old Tappan, N.J.: Revell, 1976.

Schelling, T. C. "Command and Control." In *Social Responsibility and the Business Predicament*. J. W. McKie, ed. Washington, D.C.: The Brookings Institution, 1974, pp. 79–108.

Schroeder, H., and K. V. Ramanathan. "Accounting and Corporate Accountability: An Extended Comment," *Accounting Organization and Society*, June 1984, pp. 409–15.

Shapiro, E. C., F. P. Haseltine, and M. P. Rowe. "Moving Up: Role Models, Mentors, and the 'Patron System,'" *Sloan Management Review*, Spring 1978, pp. 51–58.

Shaw, B. "Affirmative Action: An Ethical Evaluation," *Journal of Business Ethics*, October 1988, pp. 763–70.

Shockley, R. A. "Perceptions of Auditors' Independence: An Empirical Analysis," *Accounting Review*, October 1981, pp. 785–800.

Singer, P. "Rights and the Market." In *Justice and Economic Distribution*. J. Arthur and W. H. Shaw, eds. Englewood Cliffs, N.J.: Prentice-Hall, 1978, pp. 207–219.

———. *Practical Ethics*. Cambridge, Eng.: Cambridge University Press, 1979.

Skow, J. "The Myth of Male Housework," *Time*, August 7, 1989, p. 62.

Smart, J.C.C., and B. Williams. *Utilitarianism For and Against*. Cambridge, Eng.: Cambridge University Press, 1973.

Stephens, R. G., J. F. Dillard, and D. K. Dennis. "Implications of Formal Grammars for Accounting Policy Development," *Journal of Accounting and Public Policy*, Summer 1985, pp. 123–47.

Stevenson, R. W. "Workers Who Turn in Bosses Use Law to Seek Big Rewards," *New York Times*, July 10, 1989, pp. 1, 25.

Stone, C. D. "Corporate Social Responsibility: What It Might Mean, If It Were Really to Matter," *Iowa Law Review*, January 1986, pp. 557–75.

Toulmin, S. E. *An Examination of the Place of Reason in Ethics*. Cambridge, Mass.: Cambridge University Press, 1950.

Wasserstrom, R. "Lawyers as Professionals: Some Moral Issues," *Human Rights*, Fall 1975, pp. 1–24.

Wayne, L. "Where Were the Accountants?" *New York Times*, March 12, 1989, Section 3, pp. 1, 12.

_____. "Showdown at 'Gunbelt Savings,'" *New York Times*, March 12, 1989, Section 3, pp. 1, 12, 13.

Werhane, P. H. *Persons, Rights and Corporations*. Englewood Cliffs, N.J.: Prentice-Hall, 1985.

_____. "Sexual Static and the Idea of Professional Objectivity." In *It Comes with the Territory: An Inquiry Concerning Work and the Person*. A. R. Gini and T. Sullivan, eds. New York: Random House, 1989.

Westin, A., ed. *Whistle Blowing: Loyalty and Dissent in the Corporation*. New York: McGraw-Hill, 1980.

Wheeler, S., K. Mann, and A. Sarat. *Sitting in Judgement: The Sentencing of White-Collar Criminals*. New Haven: Yale University Press, 1988.

Williams, B. *Morality: An Introduction to Ethics*. New York: Harper and Row, 1972.

Williams, P. F. "The Legitimate Concern with Fairness," *Accounting Organization and Society*, March 1987, pp. 169–89.

Winch, P. *The Idea of a Social Science*. London: Routledge and Kegan Paul, 1958.

Zeff, S. A. "Does the CPA Belong to a Profession?" *Accounting Horizons*, June 1987, pp. 65–68.

Zey, M. G. *The Mentor Connection*. Homewood, Ill.: Dow Jones-Irwin, 1984.

INDEX

ABOUT THE AUTHORS

PHILIP G. COTTELL, JR., is Associate Professor of Accountancy at Miami University, Ohio, and the author of numerous articles on accounting topics.

TERRY M. PERLIN is Professor of Interdisciplinary Studies, also at Miami University, Ohio. His articles on ethical issues have appeared in publications such as *Humanistic Medicine* and *Medical Humanities Review*.